Asian Americans:

A Statistical Sourcebook

2006

Asian Americans:

A Statistical Sourcebook

2006

American Profiles Series™

information publications

Woodside, California

Also from Information Publications

State & Municipal Profiles Series™

Almanac of the 50 States

California Cities, Towns & Counties

Connecticut Municipal Profiles

Florida Municipal Profiles

Massachusetts Municipal Profiles

The New Jersey Municipal Data Book

North Carolina Municipal Profiles

American Profiles Series™

Asian Americans: A Statistical Sourcebook
Black Americans: A Statistical Sourcebook
Hispanic Americans: A Statistical Sourcebook

ISBN 0-929960-40-8
Asian Americans: A Statistical Sourcebook, 2006

Printed in the United States of America

Information Publications, Inc.
2995 Woodside Rd., Suite 400-182
Woodside, CA 94062-2446

www.informationpublications.com

Toll Free Phone 877.544.INFO (4636)
Toll Free Fax 877.544.4635

Direct Dial Phone 650.568.6170
Direct Dial Fax 650.568.6150

Chapter 9 – Vital Statistics & Health 151

Introduction

Introduction

This first edition of *Asian Americans: A Statistical Sourcebook 2006 Edition* is the newest addition to Information Publications' American Profile Series – an annual series of statistical sourcebooks covering significant topics in American life. *Asian Americans* resulted from the view that, despite the fact that there is coverage of Asian Americans in an assortment of reference sources, there is a need for a single volume statistical reference devoted entirely to this important segment of the population.

The overall goal of *Asian Americans* is to bring together into a single volume a variety of diverse information and present it, grouped by subject, in a clear, comprehensible format. It is not intended as a detailed research tool, but rather as a ready reference source, the first place to turn to find statistical information about Asian Americans.

Asian Americans provides an extensive collection of tables which display information on a wide variety of topics. With a few exceptions, each table presents information about the Asian population, the White population, and a total for Americans of all races and ethnic groups. The purpose in doing so is not to advance a specific perspective about Asian Americans but to provide a context within which the tabular data can be more fully understood and evaluated.

Presenting data by race and ethnicity always puts one at risk of being labeled racist. Although undoubtedly there will be persons on both sides - those who see *Asian Americans* as a propagandistic derogation of the Asian community and those who feel that the book eloquently proves the inherent prejudice of our culture - the intent here is to serve neither cause. In fact, *Asian Americans* is not intended to serve any cause or advance any point of view but to serve as a reportorial resource, providing access to federal government information. By researching and presenting this sometimes difficult to find, hard to understand information, *Asian Americans* can serve students, business persons, reporters, social scientists, researchers, and others who need basic data about Asian Americans.

The use of the term 'Asian' itself can also be a cause for controversy. 'Asian' is used here solely because it is the word currently used by the federal government in gathering data. In some surveys, data is further analyzed into subgroups of the Asian population (e.g., Chinese, Asian Indian, etc.). Where such data is available in this detail, it is presented here.

Another sensitive question is, who is Asian? For federal data collection purposes, Asian persons are those who say they are Asian. For statistical reporting purposes, being Asian is based solely on the self-identification of the respondent.

Organization

The main portion of this book has been divided into ten chapters of tables:

Chapter 1:	Demographics & Social Characteristics
Chapter 2:	Household & Family Characteristics
Chapter 3:	Education: Nursery through High School
Chapter 4:	Education: Postsecondary & Educational Attainment
Chapter 5:	Government & Elections
Chapter 6:	The Labor Force, Employment & Unemployment
Chapter 7:	Earnings, Income, Poverty, & Wealth
Chapter 8:	Crime & Corrections
Chapter 9:	Vital Statistics & Health
Chapter 10:	Special Topics

The tables in each chapter represent results of a comprehensive review of available federal government statistical information on the Asian population. This material was edited and organized into chapters and arranged in a sequence roughly following the pattern found in publications of the U.S. Bureau of the Census.

Each table presents pertinent information from the source or sources in a clear, comprehensible fashion. As users of this book will likely be a diverse group ranging from librarians to business planners, from social scientists to marketers, all with different uses for the same data, the information selected for presentation was chosen for its broad scope and general appeal.

The Sources

All of the information in *Asian Americans* comes from U.S. Government sources either originally or by way of republication by the federal government. In turn, most of the federal information is from the U.S. Bureau of the Census. Without question, the Bureau is the largest data gathering organization in the nation. It collects information on an exceptionally broad range of topics, not only for its own use and for the use of Congress and the Executive, but also for other federal agencies and departments. The reach of the Bureau is wider than most people realize. It encompasses the decennial Census of Population, the Current Population Survey, and the Annual Housing Survey. In cooperation with other agencies, the Bureau extends to the Consumer Expenditure Survey, the National Crime Survey, the National Family Growth Survey, and many others. The fact that the Bureau is responsible for so much of the federal government's data collection adds uniformity to the statistical information published by different agencies. Although the uniformity is not complete, there is enough to make the work of data users a lot easier. The influence of the Bureau of the Census extends beyond federal government data collection. Because of the sheer volume of data it collects, many private data collectors have adopted some of its procedures and terminology. This has the added value for researchers of making private and public data more compatible.

Observant readers will note that the source of many tables is a Census publication, *Statistical Abstract of the United States*. There are a number of reasons for this. First, due to federal budget cuts, a growing quantity of information used in *Statistical Abstract* has never been published elsewhere before or it has never been published in such a detailed way. Second, as the preeminent federal data publisher, the Census Bureau has access to a wealth of raw data in machine readable form. It is able to aggregate data geographically on regional lines and break out other detail such as age, sex, race, etc., using its own parameters for publication. Thus, even when information is published elsewhere, the manner of presentation in *Statistical Abstract* is likely to be unique. Data from this source is presented in a more general way so as to be useful to many different types of data users.

Types of Information

Regardless of its source, there are basically two types of data presented in the tables of this book.

The first is complete count data. For example, the five questions asked of all Americans by the Bureau of the Census in its decennial census was an attempt at a complete count of a given universe.

The second type of data is survey information. Here a fairly large, specifically chosen segment of a population is studied. This sample is drawn to be statistically representative of the entire population or universe. Information about housing units and money income are some of the items in this book based on this type of survey information. Of course, survey information is only as good as the survey itself; therefore, the reader should always be the judge of the significance and accuracy of the material presented as it applies to his or her own research. Although specific survey methodology is not discussed here, a full reference to each source is made on every table. Interested readers may consult the original source materials, which in most cases contain a detailed explanation of survey methodology.

The Tables

This section details how the tables have been prepared and presented. Table titles are the first source of valuable information:

Table 3.01 School Enrollment, by Age, 2004

The table number contains the chapter number to the left of the decimal and the location of the table within the chapter to the right of the decimal. Thus Table 3.01 is the first table of Chapter 3. With a few exceptions, tables have been arranged within a chapter to present the oldest, most general information first, followed by newer, more specific information. This pattern is mirrored in the tables themselves, which present the oldest, most general information at the beginning.

In a table title, the word or words before the first comma identify the general topic of the table. Following the first comma is descriptive wording which identifies the detail presented about the general topic; i.e., the data is presented by age, sex, marital status, etc., in this case, by age. After the description of the presentation of the data, the years for which data is presented are shown.

To further facilitate use, most tables in the book present data in two, three, or six columns. The left-most column or columns are for the Asian population; the center column or columns are for the White population; and the right-hand column or columns present data for all races and/or ethnic groups. For data which is available in subgroups of the Asian population, a separate table is provided, with seven columns for Asian Indian, Chinese, Filipino, Japanese, Korean, Vietnamese, and a total of all persons of Asian origin.

Along the left margin of each table appears a column of line descriptors. Here, after a general heading, subgroups of the heading (usually indented) are shown. Two principles cover arranging and presenting the line descriptors: the oldest, most general information appears first, progressing to the newer, more specific; and quantities appear first, followed by percentages, medians, means, and per capita amounts.

Wherever available and appropriate, a time span of data is presented, usually going back five to ten years. This provides readers with a historical context for the information. However, readers should be cautioned that the years selected have been chosen from no special knowledge of the subject, nor to make any specific point. Thus the fact that there has been a decrease or increase in a given indicator for the period displayed does not mean that the same trend will continue, or that it represents the continuation of a historical trend, or even that which appears to be a trend within this period actually is one. The time span and specific dates have been chosen largely to create a congruity of data, and a basis of comparison between different categories of information.

Table Notes

At the bottom of each table three key paragraphs appear: Source, Notes, and Units. The **Source** paragraph lists the source of the data presented in the table. When more than one source was used, the sources are listed in the same order in which the data itself appears in the table. As all sources are government publications, the issuing agency is listed as the author. All citations provide the table number in the source from which the material was taken.

An increasing number of sources are now available on the internet, and in many cases, only on the internet. For tables pulled exclusively from on-line sources, the Universal Resource Locator (URL) is listed as the source.

The paragraph of **Notes** includes pertinent facts about the data. One general note can be made here at the outset about all tabular data: detail (subgroups) may not add to the total shown, due to either rounding or the fact that only selected subgroups are displayed.

The final paragraph of a table, **Units,** identifies the units used, specifically stating that the quantity is millions of persons, thousands of workers, dollars per capita, etc. Readers are urged to pay special attention to this especially when a median, mean, percent, rate, or a per capita amount is provided.

The Index

Most key terms from the tables have been indexed. Readers should note that the index provides table numbers as opposed to page numbers.

The Glossary

Whenever necessary for understanding the data, specialized terms are defined either in the table or the glossary. The intention was to provide short, clear definitions, including only as much background material as necessary to make a term understandable in a general sense. For many tables, it is not possible to adequately define a term in the table notes, so the glossary serves as an important tool in using the tables.

Before drawing any conclusions from the data, however, it is absolutely vital to understand the meaning of all terms used in a table. For certain terms, some methodological background is essential in order to achieve an understanding of the material presented. Not only does the government have overtly specialized terms which clearly require a definition or explanation, but many government agencies use ordinary words in specialized ways. There are real differences between: a household and a family; a family and a married couple; the resident population and the civilian non-institutional population; a service industry and a service occupation; an urban area and a metropolitan area; to name just a few.

Readers requiring detailed definitions and an understating of the technical and methodological detail are referred to the sources for more complete explanations.

A Suggestion on How to Use This Book

One way to use this book is by locating the subject of general interest in the Table of Contents, and turning to that chapter. While the Table of Contents is detailed enough to narrow a search and the index can speed access to specific items, sometimes paging through the dozen or so tables in a given field uncovers unanticipated information of genuine importance. It is just this type of serendipity that has led to the inclusion of information in this book, and sometimes such an unexpected find can greatly enhance a research project.

Disclaimer

Asian Americans contains thousands of pieces of information. Every reasonable precaution, along with a good deal of care, was taken in its preparation. Despite all efforts it is possible that some of the information contained in this book may not be accurate. Some errors may be due to errors in the original source materials; others may have been made by the compilers of this volume. The compilers, editors, typists, printers and others are all human, and in a work of this magnitude the possibility of error can never be fully eliminated.

The publisher is also aware that some users may apply the data in this book in various remunerative projects. Although we have taken all reasonable, responsible measures to insure accuracy, we cannot take responsibility for liability or losses suffered by users of the data. The information provided here is believed to be correct at the time of publication. No other guarantees are made or implied. **The publisher assumes no liability for losses incurred by users, and warrants only the diligence and due care were used in the production of this volume.**

A Final Word

As this book is updated on an annual basis, questions, comments, and criticisms from users are vital to making informed editorial choices about succeeding editions. If you have a suggestion or comment, be assured that it will be both appreciated and carefully considered. If you should find an error here, please let us know so that it may be corrected. Our goal is to provide accurate, easy to use, statistical compendiums that serve our readers' needs. Your help enables us to do our job better.

Chapter 1: Demographics & Social Characteristics

Table 1.01 Resident Population and Median Age, 2000 and 2003-2004

	Asian		White		All Races	
	total	median age	total	median age	total	median age
2000 (April)	10,589	32.5	228,107	36.6	281,425	35.3
2003 (July)	11,925	33.7	234,196	37.3	290,810	35.9
2004 (July)	12,326	34.1	236,058	37.5	293,655	36.0

SOURCE: U.S. Bureau of the Census, Statistical Abstract of the United States, 2004-2005, table 14; 2006, table 14.

NOTES: 'All Races' includes other races and ethnic groups not shown separately.

UNITS: Population in thousands of persons; median age in years.

Table 1.02 Resident Population, by Sex, 2000 and 2004

	Asian	White	All Races
2000			
Total	10,589	228,107	281,425
Male	5,128	112,478	138,056
Female	5,461	115,628	143,368
2004			
Total	12,326	236,058	293,655
Male	5,975	116,832	144,537
Female	6,352	119,225	149,118

SOURCE: U.S. Bureau of the Census, Statistical Abstract of the United States, 2006; p. 15, table 13; (data from US. Bureau of the Census, *National Population Estimates-Characteristics*, published 9 June 2005).

NOTES: 'All Races' includes other races and ethnic groups not shown separately.

UNITS: Resident population in thousands of persons.

Table 1.03 Resident Population, by Age, 2000 and 2004

	Asian	White	All Races
2000			
Total	10,589	228,107	281,425
under 5 years old	708	14,663	19,185
5-13 years old	1,288	28,384	37,028
14-17 years old	590	12,524	16,094
18-24 years old	1,178	21,195	27,139
65 years and older	815	30,959	34,986
85 years old and older	63	3,825	4,237
2004			
Total	12,326	236,058	293,655
under 5 years old	824	15,345	20,071
5-13 years old	1,399	27,754	36,376
14-17 years old	627	12,935	16,831
18 to 24 years old	1,235	22,734	29,245
65 years and older	1,048	31,770	36,294
85 years old and older	97	4,366	4,860

SOURCE: U.S. Bureau of the Census, Statistical Abstract of the United States, 2006; p. 16, table 14; (data from US. Bureau of the Census, *National Population Estimates-Characteristics*, published 9 June 2005).

NOTES: 'All Races' includes other races and ethnic groups not shown separately.

UNITS: Resident population in thousands of persons.

Table 1.04 Population, by Age and Residence Region, 2004

	Asian	White	All Races
Age			
Persons of all ages			
persons:	12,301	233,702	290,605
under 18 years old	2,870	56,079	73,271
18-24 years old	1,113	21,855	27,972
25-34 years old	2,249	30,782	39,307
35-44 years old	2,175	34,759	43,350
45-54 years old	1,708	34,526	41,960
55-59 years old	653	14,120	16,763
60-64 years old	442	10,871	12,769
65 years old and over	1,092	30,710	35,213
Residence			
Northeast	2,484	44,067	53,910
Midwest	1,531	55,175	64,743
South	2,531	79,915	104,878
West	5,754	54,545	67,075

SOURCE: U.S. Bureau of the Census, Current Population Reports: Poverty in the United States: 2004; "Table POV01: Age and Sex of All People, Family Members and Unrelated Individuals Iterated by Income-to-Poverty Ratio and Race: 2004, Below 100% of Poverty"; "Table POV41: Region, Division and Type of Residence – Poverty Status for All People, Family Members and Unrelated Individuals by Family Structure: 2004, Below 100% of Poverty".

NOTES: 'All Races' includes other races not shown separately. 'White' as shown is equivalent to 'White Alone' that refers to people who reported 'White' did not report any other race category.

UNITS: Population in thousands of persons.

Table 1.05 Resident Population, by Region, 2000

	Asian Indian	Chinese	Filipino	Japanese	Korean	Vietnamese	Total Asian
Population:							
United States	1,679	2,433	1,850	797	1,077	1,123	10,243
Northeast	554	692	202	76	246	115	2,119
Midwest	293	212	151	63	132	107	1,198
South	441	343	245	77	224	336	1,922
West	391	1,186	1,253	580	474	564	5,004
Percent Distribution							
United States	100%	100%	100%	100%	100%	100%	100%
Northeast	33.0	28.4	10.9	9.6	22.9	10.3	20.7
Midwest	17.5	8.7	8.2	7.9	12.3	9.5	11.7
South	26.3	14.1	13.2	9.7	20.8	29.9	18.8
West	23.3	48.8	67.7	72.8	44.0	50.3	48.8

SOURCE: U.S. Bureau of the Census, Statistical Abstract of the United States, 2006; p. 28, table 24; (data from US. Census Bureau, "Demographic Profies: Census 2000.").

NOTES: 'Total Asian' includes other races and ethnic groups not shown separately.

UNITS: Resident population in thousands of persons.

Table 1.06 Resident Population, by State, 2004 (estimate)

	Asian Indian	Chinese	Filipino	Japanese	Korean	Viet-namese	Total Asian
Alabama	4,551	5,210	1,929	2,448	5,225	13,090	33,570
Alaska	433	1,204	12,649	2,467	3,910	228	27,970
Arizona	32,858	19,246	20,200	7,954	8,498	19,149	123,766
Arkansas	5,606	3,922	1,198	352	1,260	5,961	25,294
California	405,976	1,098,233	1,059,512	315,549	411,062	495,142	4,256,198
Colorado	15,162	17,879	6,218	13,885	24,964	17,522	113,570
Connecticut	29,075	23,110	10,056	7,695	11,133	6,521	102,377
Delaware	6,242	4,119	4,914	304	1,789	1,782	22,264
District of Columbia	4,243	2,819	2,073	1,752	1,373	1,270	15,244
Florida	11,165	55,220	61,743	16,218	21,731	34,295	348,112
Georgia	52,486	40,183	17,282	12,362	40,178	29,762	238,281
Hawaii	1,255	51,144	188,759	206,331	25,382	9,833	524,613
Idaho	2,546	3,590	1,027	2,475	3,022	1,264	15,656
Illinois	152,598	82,504	106,909	21,576	73,151	14,736	502,263
Indiana	17,602	15,759	7,835	4,771	9,388	6,503	65,891
Iowa	3,939	9,096	3,228	323	2,423	4,007	35,056
Kansas	6,656	8,399	7,068	2,261	5,129	13,433	56,701
Kentucky	6,113	7,940	3,127	2,834	5,493	6,076	35,164
Louisiana	8,390	11,411	2,933	1,370	3,492	20,861	58,035
Maine	1,452	1,077	2,155	1,106	451	527	9,182
Maryland	69,608	62,198	25,440	7,616	39,492	16,030	254,393
Massachusetts	62,661	110,514	10,792	11,894	14,836	40,743	283,635
Michigan	93,681	31,148	21,436	9,908	26,624	11,780	219,855
Minnesota	19,508	24,118	6,897	5,517	22,550	15,729	176,182
Mississippi	4,083	1,559	2,656	405	1,266	373	10,811
Missouri	12,967	17,096	8,845	1,850	9,918	7,743	67,518
Montana	364	543	1,246	496	431	0	3,395

continued on the next page

Table 1.06 continued

	Asian Indian	Chinese	Filipino	Japanese	Korean	Viet-namese	Total Asian
Nebraska	2,464	4,645	3,185	675	3,568	6,846	24,707
Nevada	5,739	17,569	58,647	12,220	12,115	10,067	130,681
New Hampshire	5,268	4,739	2,799	307	2,604	2,364	21,973
New Jersey	229,994	132,533	92,009	9,420	70,825	29,367	601,939
New Mexico	3,685	4,775	3,738	3,150	3,588	1,004	24,705
New York	317,375	502,760	99,021	34,060	128,256	25,563	1,215,205
North Carolina	36,056	24,098	13,594	3,046	23,195	15,192	139
North Dakota	1,158	592	947	153	286	514	4,147
Ohio	45,787	36,246	18,299	9,537	16,433	13,975	159,146
Oklahoma	11,491	4,810	6,168	4,686	5,582	14,318	52,311
Oregon	8,795	23,702	15,426	12,631	12,424	28,426	123,018
Pennsylvania	77,172	68,879	15,062	6,178	21,129	41,107	258,591
Rhode Island	5,267	3,703	2,130	691	1,517	2,512	27,930
South Carolina	8,052	7,526	8,451	2,011	6,099	5,116	43,842
South Dakota	755	817	1,183	367	367	1,408	5,371
Tennessee	17,280	10,763	7,301	3,331	9,168	8,204	72,931
Texas	182,361	126,420	72,179	19,377	54,025	153,691	701,483
Utah	9,936	7,799	4,987	4,051	2,418	5,171	46,132
Vermont	1,750	546	19	620	1,055	1,224	5,671
Virginia	80,530	50,217	50,546	6,397	45,358	45,483	326,563
Washington	41,144	73,108	67,330	34,011	47,809	56,079	318,867
West Virginia	1,977	1,430	1,344	397	316	355	7,128
Wisconsin	19,403	12,177	4,953	2,497	8,333	4,975	94,414
Wyoming	180	532	782	407	451	189	3,108

SOURCE: U.S. Bureau of the Census, Statistical Abstract of the United States,

NOTES: 'Total Asian' includes other races and ethnic groups not shown separately.

Table 1.07 Foreign-Born Population, by Age, 2004

	Asian	All Races
Total	8,685	34,244
under 5 years old	86	334
5 - 14 years old	339	1,822
15 - 24 years old	894	4,561
25 - 34 years old	1,843	7,784
35 - 44 years old	2,007	7,559
45 - 54 years old	1,587	5,316
55 - 64 years old	989	3,171
65 - 74 years old	593	2,092
75 - 84 years old	262	1,231
85 years old and over	85	374

SOURCE: U.S. Bureau of the Census, Statistical Abstract of the United States, 2006; p. 45, table 43; (data from US. Bureau of the Census, *Foreign-Born Population of the United States Current Population Survey – March 2004 Detailed Tables (PPL-176)* published February 2005).

NOTES: 'All Races' includes other races and ethnic groups not shown separately.

UNITS: Population in thousands of persons.

Table 1.08 Foreign-Born Population, by Citizenship Status, 2003

	Asian	All Races
Total	9,147	33,534
naturalized citizen	4,917	13,896
not U.S. citizen		
number	4,230	19,640
percent	46%	59%

SOURCE: U.S. Bureau of the Census, Statistical Abstract of the United States, 2006; p. 45, table 44; (data from US. Bureau of the Census, *Foreign-Born Population of the United States Current Population Survey – March 2004 Detailed Tables (PPL-176)* published February 2005).

NOTES: 'All Races' includes other races and ethnic groups not shown separately.

UNITS: Population in thousands of persons.

Table 1.09 Population Projections, 2000 - 2050 (revised)

	Asian	White	All Races
Population, total			
2000	10,684	228,548	282,125
2010	14,241	244,995	308,936
2020	17,988	260,629	335,805
2030	22,580	275,731	363,584
2040	27,992	289,690	391,946
2050	33,430	302,626	419,854
Percent of total population			
2000	3.8%	81.0%	100%
2010	4.6	79.3	100%
2020	5.4	77.6	100%
2030	6.2	75.8	100%
2040	7.1	73.9	100%
2050	8.0	72.1	100%

SOURCE: U.S. Bureau of the Census, "Projected Population of the United States by Race, and Hispanic Origin: 2000 to 2050", Table 1a (data from "U.S. Interim Projections by Age, Sex, Race, and Hispanic Origin," <http://www.census.gov/ipc/www/usinterimproj/>, Internet release date: 18 March, 2004).

NOTES: 'All Races' includes other races and ethnic groups not shown separately. Population projections as of July 1, of the year shown. 'Asian' and 'White' as shown are equivalent to 'Asian Alone' and 'White Alone' respectively.

UNITS: Estimates of the All Races population in thousands of persons, includes armed forces overseas.

Table 1.10 Population Projections, by Age, 2005 and 2010

	Asian	White	All Races
2005			
total	12,419	236,924	295,507
under 5 years	833	15,503	20,495
5 to 9 years	763	14,862	19,467
10 to 14 years	787	15,881	20,838
15 to 19 years	815	16,281	21,272
20 to 24 years	898	16,153	20,823
25 to 29 years	985	15,377	19,753
30 to 34 years	1,190	15,466	19,847
35 to 39 years	1,117	16,538	20,869
40 to 44 years	1,033	18,318	22,735
45 to 49 years	948	18,312	22,453
50 to 54 years	828	16,499	19,983
55 to 59 years	685	14,582	17,359
60 to 64 years	480	11,075	13,017
65 to 69 years	370	8,629	10,123
70 to 74 years	275	7,348	8,500
75 to 79 years	200	6,506	7,376
80 to 84 years	125	4,993	5,576
85 to 89 years	59	2,890	3,206
90 to 94 years	22	1,286	1,431
95 to 99 years	5	366	412
100 years old and over	1	60	71

continued on the next page

Table 1.10 continued

	Asian	White	All Races
2010			
total	14,241	244,995	308,936
under 5 years	919	15,995	21,426
5 to 9 years	888	15,639	20,706
10 to 14 years	834	15,049	19,767
15 to 19 years	886	16,203	21,336
20 to 24 years	943	16,591	21,676
25 to 29 years	1,041	16,495	21,375
30 to 34 years	1,166	15,654	20,271
35 to 39 years	1,319	15,597	20,137
40 to 44 years	1,208	16,566	20,984
45 to 49 years	1,105	18,213	22,654
50 to 54 years	997	18,066	22,173
55 to 59 years	857	16,102	19,507
60 to 64 years	706	14,004	16,679
65 to 69 years	489	10,357	12,172
70 to 74 years	355	7,767	9,097
75 to 79 years	244	6,226	7,186
80 to 84 years	158	5,005	5,665
85 to 89 years	83	3,321	3,713
90 to 94 years	31	1,546	1,727
95 to 99 years	8	503	569
100 years old and over	1	98	114

SOURCE: U.S. Bureau of the Census, Statistical Abstract of the United States, 2006; p. 17, table 15; (data from US. Bureau of the Census, *U.S. Interim Projections by Age, Sex, Race and Hispanic Origin*, published March 2004).

NOTES: 'All Races' includes other races and ethnic groups not shown separately. Population projections as of July 1, of the year shown.

UNITS: Estimates of the total population in thousands of persons, includes armed forces overseas.

Table 1.11 Population, Projected Change, 2000 - 2050

	Asian	White	All Races
Numerical Change:			
2000 - 2050	22,746	74,078	137,729
by decade:			
2000 - 2010	3,557	16,447	26,811
2010 - 2020	3,747	15,634	26,869
2020 - 2030	4,592	15,102	27,779
2030 - 2040	5,412	13,959	28,362
2040 - 2050	5,438	12,936	27,908
Percent Change			
2000 - 2050	212.9%	32.4%	48.8%
by decade:			
2000 - 2010	33.3	7.2	9.5
2010 - 2020	26.3	6.4	8.7
2020 - 2030	25.5	5.8	8.3
2030 - 2040	24.0	5.1	7.8
2040 - 2050	19.4	4.5	7.1

SOURCE: U.S. Bureau of the Census, "Projected Population of the United States by Race, and Hispanic Origin: 2000 to 2050", Table 1b (data from "U.S. Interim Projections by Age, Sex, Race, and Hispanic Origin," <http://www.census.gov/ipc/www/usinterimproj/>, Internet release date: 18 March, 2004).

NOTES: 'All Races' includes other races and ethnic groups not shown separately. Population projections as of July 1, of the year shown. 'Asian' and 'White' as shown are equivalent to 'Asian Alone' and 'White Alone' respectively.

UNITS: Estimates of the total population in thousands of persons, includes armed forces overseas.

Table 1.12 Marital Status, Persons 15 Years Old and Older, 2000 - 2005

	Asian		White		All Races	
	number	percent	number	percent	number	percent
Both Sexes:						
2000						
All marital statuses	8,415	100.0%	177,581	100.0%	213,773	100.0%
married, spouse present	4,511	53.6	99,258	55.9	113,002	52.9
married, spouse absent	284	3.4	1,971	1.1	2,730	1.3
widowed	337	4.0	11,532	6.5	13,665	6.4
divorced	360	4.3	16,547	9.3	19,881	9.3
separated	137	1.6	2,976	1.7	4,479	2.1
never married	2,787	33.1	45,297	25.5	60,016	28.1
2005*						
All marital statuses	9,930	100.0%	187,550	100.0%	230,261	100.0%
married, spouse present	5,732	57.7	102,435	54.6	119,026	51.7
married, spouse absent	311	3.1	2,567	1.4	3,554	1.5
widowed	402	4.1	11,527	6.1	13,836	6.0
divorced	500	5.0	18,109	9.7	22,186	9.6
separated	153	1.5	3,339	1.8	4,824	2.1
never married	2,831	28.5	49,574	26.4	66,835	29.0

SOURCE: U.S. Bureau of the Census, Current Population Reports: America's Families and Living Arrangements: 2000; Series P-20, #537, table A1, issued June 2001; 2005; "Table A1. Marital Status of People 15 Years and Over, by Age, Sex, Personal Earnings, Race, and Hispanic Origin: March 2005", issued May 2006. <www.census.gov>

NOTES: 'All Races' includes other races and ethnic groups not shown separately. '*' denotes that 'White' and 'Asian' as shown are equivalent to 'White Alone' and 'Asian Alone', respectively.

UNITS: Number in thousands of persons 15 years old and older; percent as a percent of total (percents **not** standardized for age).

Table 1.13 Marital Status, Men 15 Years Old and Older, 2000 - 2005

	Asian		White		All Races	
	number	percent	number	percent	number	percent
Men:						
2000						
All marital statuses	4,041	100.0%	86,443	100.0%	103,114	100.0%
married, spouse present	2,118	52.4	49,672	57.5	56,501	54.8
married, spouse absent	163	4.0	979	1.1	1,365	1.3
widowed	49	1.2	2,196	2.5	2,604	2.5
divorced	130	3.2	7,246	8.4	8,572	8.3
separated	53	1.3	1,237	1.4	1,818	1.8
never married	1,528	37.8	25,113	29.1	32,253	31.3
2005*						
All marital statuses	4,749	100.0%	91,777	100.0%	111,584	100.0%
married, spouse present	2,675	56.3	51,277	55.9	59,513	53.3
married, spouse absent	161	3.4	1,451	1.6	1,919	1.7
widowed	70	1.5	2,289	2.5	2,725	2.4
divorced	182	3.8	7,661	8.3	9,220	8.3
separated	61	1.3	1,343	1.5	1,936	1.7
never married	1,600	33.7	27,755	30.2	36,271	32.5

SOURCE: U.S. Bureau of the Census, Current Population Reports: America's Families and Living Arrangements: 2000; Series P-20, #537, table A1, issued June 2001; 2005; "Table A1. Marital Status of People 15 Years and Over, by Age, Sex, Personal Earnings, Race, and Hispanic Origin: March 2005", issued May 2006. <www.census.gov>

NOTES: 'All Races' includes other races and ethnic groups not shown separately. '*' denotes that 'White' and 'Asian' as shown are equivalent to 'White Alone' and 'Asian Alone', respectively.

UNITS: Number in thousands of men 15 years old and older; percent as a percent of total (percents **not** standardized for age).

Table 1.14 Marital Status, Women 15 Years Old and Older, 2000 - 2005

	Asian		White		All Races	
	number	percent	number	percent	number	percent
Women:						
2000						
All marital statuses	4,374	100.0%	91,138	100.0%	110,660	100.0%
married, spouse present	2,393	54.7	49,586	54.4	56,501	51.1
married, spouse absent	120	2.8	992	1.1	1,365	1.2
widowed	287	6.6	9,336	10.2	11,061	10.0
divorced	230	5.3	9,301	10.2	11,309	10.2
separated	84	1.9	1,739	1.9	2,661	2.4
never married	1,259	28.8	20,184	22.1	27,763	25.1
2005*						
All marital statuses	5,181	100.0%	95,773	100.0%	118,678	100.0%
married, spouse present	3,057	59.0	51,158	53.4	59,513	50.1
married, spouse absent	150	2.9	1,116	1.2	1,635	1.4
widowed	333	6.4	9,238	9.6	11,111	9.4
divorced	318	6.1	10,448	10.9	12,966	10.9
separated	92	1.8	1,996	2.1	2,889	2.4
never married	1,231	23.8	21,819	22.8	30,565	25.8

SOURCE: U.S. Bureau of the Census, Current Population Reports: America's Families and Living Arrangements: 2000; Series P-20, #537, table A1, issued June 2001; 2005; "Table A1. Marital Status of People 15 Years and Over, by Age, Sex, Personal Earnings, Race, and Hispanic Origin: March 2005", issued May 2006. <www.census.gov>

NOTES: 'All Races' includes other races and ethnic groups not shown separately. '*' denotes that 'White' and 'Asian' as shown are equivalent to 'White Alone' and 'Asian Alone', respectively.

UNITS: Number in thousands of women 15 years old and older; percent as a percent of total (percents **not** standardized for age).

Table 1.15 Children Who Speak a Language Other Than English at Home, 2000 - 2003

	Asian	White	All Races
2000			
Total number (mil.)	na	na	9.5
percent of children 5-17 yrs who:			
speak another language at home	67.1%	5.7%	18.1%
have difficulty speaking English	19.8	1.3	5.5
2001			
Total number (mil.)	na	na	9.8
percent of children 5-17 yrs who:			
speak another language at home	66.6%	5.7%	18.5%
have difficulty speaking English	20.5	1.4	5.4
2002			
Total number (mil.)	na	na	9.8
percent of children 5-17 yrs who:			
speak another language at home	64.4%	5.6%	18.5%
have difficulty speaking English	18.7	1.3	5.3
2003			
Total number (mil.)	na	na	9.9
percent of children 5-17 yrs who:			
speak another language at home	63.5%	5.1%	18.6%
have difficulty speaking English	17.5	1.4	5.4

SOURCE: U.S. Bureau of the Census, Statistical Abstract of the United States, 2006; table 222.

NOTES: 'All Races' includes other races and ethnic groups not shown separately.

UNITS: Number in millions of children 5 to 17 years old.

Table 1.16 Volunteers, by Type of Organization, 2004

	Asian	White	All Races
Number of volunteers	1,832	55,892	64,542
percent of population	19.3%	30.5%	28.8%
median annual hours	40	52	52
percent by type of organization:			
civic and political	4.3%	7.2%	7.0%
educational/youth service	29.0	26.8	27.0
environmental/animal care	0.7	1.8	1.7
hospital/health	6.8	7.9	7.5
public safety	0.4	1.6	1.5
religious	34.2	33.5	34.4
social/community service	15.2	12.5	12.4
sport and hobby	5.1	3.7	3.6
other	2.1	3.4	3.3
not determined	2.1	1.5	1.6

SOURCE: U.S. Bureau of the Census, Statistical Abstract of the United States: 2006; p. 381, table 575.

NOTES: 'All Races' includes other races and ethnic groups not shown separately. 'White' and 'Asian' as shown are equivalent to 'White Alone' and 'Asian Alone', respectively; does not include persons who selected more than one race. 'Median annual hours' for those reporting annual hours.

UNITS: Number of volunteers in thousands. Percent of the volunteer population by type of organization; totals to 100%.

Chapter 2: Household & Family Characteristics

Table 2.01 Living Arrangements of Persons 15 Years or Older, 2004

	Asian	White	All Races
Total	9,577	185,742	227,343
living alone	781	24,094	29,586
living with spouse	5,554	101,812	118,128
living with other persons	3,242	59,836	79,629

SOURCE: U.S. Bureau of the Census, Statistical Abstract of the United States, 2006; p. 50, table 52.

NOTES: 'All Races' includes other races not shown separately. 'White' as shown is equivalent to 'White Alone' that refers to people who reported 'White' did not report any other race category.

UNITS: Population in thousands of persons.

Table 2.02 Selected Characteristics of Households, 2004

	Asian	White	All Races
Marital status and type of householder			
All households, both sexes	4,140	92,702	113,146
family households	3,155	63,222	77,010
married couple families	2,560	50,260	58,109
male householder, no spouse present	248	3,726	4,893
female householder, no spouse present	347	9,236	14,009
non-family households	985	29,479	36,136
male householder	466	13,371	16,344
-living alone	346	10,213	12,652
female householder	519	16,109	19,792
-living alone	428	13,935	17,207
Age of the householder			
All ages	4,140	92,702	113,146
15-24 years old	247	5,091	6,686
25-34 years old	934	15,003	19,255
35-44 years old	1,095	18,552	23,226
45-54 years old	786	19,106	23,370
55-64 years old	569	14,714	17,476
65 years old and over	509	20,234	23,135

continued on the next page

Table 2.02 continued

	Asian	White	All Races
Size of the household			
All household sizes	4,140	92,702	113,146
one person	774	24,148	29,859
two persons	1,114	31,735	37,247
three persons	852	14,615	18,347
four persons	818	13,413	16,506
five persons	334	5,847	7,230
six persons	131	1,895	2,522
seven or more persons	116	1,048	1,435
Residence			
All residences	4,140	92,702	113,146
Northeast	865	17,569	21,137
Midwest	481	22,428	25,911
South	823	32,056	41,159
West	1,970	20,649	24,939

SOURCE: U.S. Bureau of the Census, Current Population Reports: Income 2004, "(Table) HINC-01. Selected Characteristics of Households, by Total Money Income in 2004".

NOTES: 'All Races' includes other races not shown separately. 'White' as shown is equivalent to 'White alone' that refers to people who reported White and did not report any other race category.

UNITS: Number of households in thousands of households.

Table 2.03 Households With Computers and Internet Access, 2000

	Asian	White	All Races
Total households	3,457	78,719	105,247
percent			
with computers	65.1%	55.7%	51.0%
with internet access	56.2	46.1	41.5

SOURCE: U.S. Bureau of the Census, Current Population Reports: Home Computers and Internet Use in the United States: August 2000; Series P23-207; p. 3, table A.

NOTES: 'Asian' as shown is equivalent to 'Asian and Pacific Islander'. 'White' includes non-hispanic White only.

UNITS: Numbers in Thousands.

Table 2.04 Living Arrangements of Children Under 18 Years of Age, 2000 and 2005

	Asian children	White children	All children
2000			
Living with both parents	2,454	42,497	49,795
Living with mother only	428	9,765	16,162
Living with father only	76	2,427	3,058
Living with neither parent	88	1,752	2,981
2005*			
Living with both parents	2,394	41,393	49,573
Living with mother only	292	10,340	17,172
Living with father only	102	2,630	3,486
Living with neither parent	72	1,897	3,293

SOURCE: U.S. Bureau of the Census, Current Population Reports: America's Families and Living Arrangements: 2000; Series P-20, #537, pp. 1, 25, 37, and 60, table C2, issued June 2001; 2005; "Table C2. Household Relationship and Living Arrangements of Children Under 18 Years, by Age, Sex, Race, Hispanic Origin, and Metropolitan Residence: March 2005"; issued May 2006. <www.census.gov>

NOTES: 'All children' includes children of other races not shown separately. * denotes that 'White' and 'Asian' as shown are equivalent to 'White Alone' and 'Asian Alone', respectively. Otherwise, 'Asian' is equivalent to 'Asian and Pacific Islander."

UNITS: Thousands of children.

Table 2.05 Single Parents Living With Own Children Under 18 Years Old, 2000 and 2005

	Asian	White	All Races
2000			
Single Fathers			
with own children under 18	49	1,622	2,044
with own children under 12	39	1,145	1,441
with own children under 6	19	647	819
with own children under 3	39	393	511
with own children under 1	na	152	196
Single Mothers			
with own children under 18	236	6,216	9,681
with own children under 12	151	4,558	7,337
with own children under 6	59	2,519	4,115
with own children under 3	203	1,396	2,319
with own children under 1	8	499	824
2005*			
Single Fathers			
with own children under 18	62	1,913	2,487
with own children under 12	34	1,323	1,743
with own children under 6	16	762	1,026
with own children under 3	9	451	604
with own children under 1	4	176	229
Single Mothers			
with own children under 18	224	6,796	10,411
with own children under 12	142	4,882	7,621
with own children under 6	79	2,768	4,435
with own children under 3	39	1,508	2,400
with own children under 1	8	563	866

SOURCE: U.S. Bureau of the Census, Current Population Reports: America's Families and Living Arrangements: 2000; Series P-20, #537, p. 8, table 4, issued June 2001; 2005; "Table FG5. One-Parent Family Groups with Own Children Under 18, by Labor Force Status, Race, and Hispanic Origin of the Reference Person: March 2005"; issued May 2006. <www.census.gov>

NOTES: 'All Races' includes children of other races not shown separately. * denotes that 'White' and 'Asian' as shown are equivalent to 'White Alone' and 'Asian Alone', respectively. Otherwise, 'Asian' is equivalent to 'Asian and Pacific Islander."

UNITS: Thousands of fathers or mothers.

Table 2.06 Selected Characteristics of Family Households, 2003

	Asian	White	All Races
Type of family			
All families	3,155	63,227	77,019
married couple families	2,560	50,265	58,118
male householder, no wife present	248	3,726	4,893
female householder, no husband present	347	9,236	14,009
Size of family			
All family sizes	3,155	63,227	77,019
two persons	986	28,776	33,894
three persons	821	13,709	17,236
four persons	798	12,709	15,637
five persons	320	5,397	6,699
six persons	125	1,720	2,301
seven or more persons	104	916	1,252

continued on the next page

Table 2.06 continued

	Asian	White	All Races
Number of earners			
All families	3,155	63,227	77,019
no earner	255	9,041	10,972
one earner	1,053	19,324	24,671
two earners	1,455	27,864	33,116
three earners	275	5,354	6,357
four earners or more	116	1,645	1,903
Residence			
All residences	3,155	63,227	77,019
Northeast	657	11,675	14,059
Midwest	382	15,285	17,542
South	639	22,195	28,362
West	1,476	14,071	17,056

SOURCE: U.S. Bureau of the Census, Current Population Reports: Income 2004, "(Table) FINC-01. Selected Characteristics of Families by Total Money Income in 2004".

NOTES: All Races' includes other races not shown separately. Number of families as of March of the following year. 'White' as shown is equivalent to 'White Alone' that refers to people who reported 'White' and did not report any other race category. 'Number of earners' excludes families with members in the armed forces.

UNITS: Number of households in thousands of family households.

Table 2.07 Children Ages 3 - 17 Years With Access to a Home Computer and the Internet, 2000

	Asian	White	All Races
Total number of children 3 to 17 years old	2,581	38,438	60,635
percent			
home computer access	71.9%	77.3%	65.0%
use internet at home	35.2	38.4	30.4

SOURCE: U.S. Bureau of the Census, Current Population Reports: Home Computers and Internet Use in the United States: August 2000; Series P23-207; p. 4, table B.

NOTES: 'Asian' as shown is equivalent to 'Asian and Pacific Islander'. 'White' includes non-hispanic White only.

UNITS: Numbers in thousands.

Table 2.08 Primary Child Care Arrangements Used for Preschoolers by Families With Employed Mothers, Spring 1999 and Winter 2002

	Asian children	White children	All children
Spring 1999			
All preschoolers with employed mothers	339	8,411	10,587
Designated parent	5.3%	3.4%	3.2%
Other parent	12.4	20.4	19.3
Grandparent	49.6	19.4	21.7
Other relative or sibling	9.4	7.8	8.4
Daycare center	6.5	18.0	18.7
Nursery/preschool	5.4	4.1	4.0
Head start	na	0.2	0.4
Family day care	3.0	13.2	11.4
Other non-relative	5.5	10.2	9.7
Winter 2002			
All preschoolers with employed mothers	448	7,699	9,823
Designated parent	3.0%	3.6%	3.3%
Other parent	18.7	19.0	18.2
Sibling	1.0	0.5	1.0
Grandparent	23.8	18.5	19.4
Other relative	4.3	4.6	5.4
Daycare center	16.7	18.6	19.0
Nursery/preschool	9.4	5.0	5.3
Head start	na	0.7	0.8
Family day care	8.4	9.5	9.2
Other non-relative	8.2	9.6	9.0

SOURCE: U.S. Bureau of the Census, Current Population Reports: Who's Minding the Kids? Child Care Arrangements: Spring 1999; Series PPL-168; "(table 2B) Primary Child Care Arrangements of Preschoolers Living with Employed Mothers by Selected Characteristics: Spring 1999"; Winter 2002; Series P70-101.

NOTES: 'All children' includes children of other races not shown separately. Because of multiple arrangements, numbers and percentages may exceed the total number of children. 'Designated parent' is selected in households where both parents are present to report child care arrangements for each child.

UNITS: Thousands of children living in family households.

Table 2.09 Average Weekly Child Care Expenditures of Families with Employed Mothers: Winter 2002

	Asian	White	All Families
Families with children under 5 years	228	3,522	4,475
average weekly child care expenditures	$139	$127	$122
average monthly family income	$10,361	$5,648	$5,598
percent of family's monthly income spent on child care	5.8%	9.8%	9.5%
average monthly mother's income	$5,154	$2,531	$2,577
ratio of child care expenditures to mother's income	11.7	21.8	20.5
Families with children under 5 to 14 years	191	4,351	5,372
average weekly child care expenditures	$77	$85	$84
average monthly family income	$7,628	$5,941	$5,762
percent of family's monthly income spent on child care	4.4%	6.2%	6.3%
average monthly mother's income	$2,852	$2,874	$2,796
ratio of child care expenditures to mother's income	11.8	12.8	13.0

SOURCE: U.S. Bureau of the Census, Current Population Reports: Who's Minding the Kids? Child Care Arrangements: Winter 2002; Series P70-101; "(table 6) Average Weekly Child Care Expenditures of Families with Employed Mothers that Make Payments, by Age Groups and Selected Characteristics: Winter 2002"; issued November, 2005.

NOTES: 'All families' includes families of other races not shown separately. 'Asian' as shown is equivalent to 'Asian and Pacific Islander'.

UNITS: Families in Thousands.

Chapter 3: Education - Nursery through High School

Table 3.01 School Enrollment, by Age, 2004

	enrollment			enrollment rate		
	Asian	White	All Races	Asian	White	All Races
2004						
all persons 3 years and over	3,409	57,585	75,461	29.3%	25.7%	27.2%
persons 3 and 4 years old	169	3,376	4,552	58.3	52.8	54.0
persons 5 and 6 years old	313	5,784	7,561	97.2	95.5	95.4
persons 7 to 9 years old	447	8,753	11,510	99.9	98.1	98.1
persons 10 and 13 years old	628	12,560	16,496	99.1	98.3	98.6
persons 14 and 15 years old	291	6,403	8,327	97.5	98.5	98.5
persons 16 and 17 years old	338	6,188	8,086	98.6	94.2	94.5
persons 18 and 19 years old	212	3,919	4,961	82.6	64.9	64.4
persons 20 and 21 years old	245	3,094	3,904	79.7	49.3	48.9
persons 22 to 24 years old	275	2,422	3,221	46.8	25.3	26.3
persons 25 to 29 years old	220	1,835	2,479	21.5	12.2	13.0
persons 30 to 34 years old	116	993	1,321	9.5	6.4	6.6
persons 35 to 44 years old	98	1,254	1,682	4.7	3.6	3.9
persons 45 to 54 years old	43	738	979	2.5	2.2	2.4
persons 55 years and over	15	267	371	0.7	0.5	0.6

SOURCE: U.S. Bureau of the Census, Current Population Reports: School Enrollment, 2004; "(Table) 1. Enrollment Status of the Population 3 Years Old and Over, by Age, Sex, Race, Hispanic 1 Origin, Nativity, and Selected Educational Characteristics: October 2004", published October 2005.

NOTES: 'All Races' includes other races not shown separately. 'White' and 'Asian' as shown are equivalent to 'White Alone' and 'Asian Alone', respectively.

UNITS: Enrollment in thousands of persons enrolled. All years: rate as a percent of the civilian non-institutionalized population, by age group.

Table 3.02 School Enrollment by Level and Control of School, 2004

	Asian	White	All Races
Total enrolled	2,202	44,014	57,810
public	1,985	37,673	50,321
private	217	6,341	7,489
nursery school	165	3,566	4,739
public	72	1,703	2,487
private	93	1,863	2,252
kindergarten	164	3,043	3,992
public	152	2,571	3,417
private	12	472	575
elementary school	1,235	24,742	32,521
public	1,149	21,859	29,132
private	86	2,883	3,389
high school	637	12,663	16,557
public	612	11,540	15,285
private	26	1,123	1,272

SOURCE: U.S. Bureau of the Census, Current Population Reports: School Enrollment, 2004; "(Table) 5. Enrollment Below College for People 3 to 24 Years Old, By Control of School, Sex, Metropolitan Status, Race and Hispanic Origin: October 2004"; released October, 2005.

NOTES: 'All Races' includes other races not shown separately. 'White' and 'Asian' as shown equivalent to 'White Alone' and 'Asian Alone', respectively.

UNITS: Enrollment in thousands of persons enrolled; civilian non-institutionalized population.

Table 3.03 Estimates of the School Age Population, by Age and Sex, 2004

	Asian	White	All Races
Both sexes			
3 years old and over	11,621	223,841	277,467
3 and 4 years old	291	6,400	8,427
5 and 6 years old	322	6,059	7,928
7 to 9 years old	447	8,919	11,728
10-13 years old	634	12,774	16,739
14 and 15 years old	298	6,502	8,453
16 and 17 years old	343	6,569	8,556
18 and 19 years old	257	6,043	7,701
20 and 21 years old	307	6,282	7,976
22 to 24 years old	588	9,572	12,271
25 to 29 years old	1,024	14,985	19,125
30 to 34 years old	1,223	15,608	19,864
35 to 44 years old	2,076	34,741	43,142
45 to 54 years old	1,695	34,190	41,515
55 years old and over	2,118	55,200	64,042
Male			
3 years old and over	5,622	110,209	135,510
3 and 4 years old	154	3,312	4,431
5 and 6 years old	196	3,105	4,098
7 to 9 years old	196	4,576	5,967
10-13 years old	348	6,694	8,743
14 and 15 years old	145	3,180	4,119
16 and 17 years old	171	3,373	4,388
18 and 19 years old	133	3,062	3,861
20 and 21 years old	160	3,193	4,004
22 to 24 years old	292	4,852	6,153
25 to 29 years old	495	7,625	9,555
30 to 34 years old	596	7,872	9,836
35 to 44 years old	1,006	17,357	21,221
45 to 54 years old	786	16,931	20,293
55 years old and over	942	25,078	28,842

continued on the next page

Table 3.03 continued

	Asian	White	All Races
Female			
3 years old and over	5,999	113,632	141,957
3 and 4 years old	136	3,088	3,997
5 and 6 years old	125	2,954	3,830
7 to 9 years old	251	4,343	5,761
10-13 years old	285	6,080	7,996
14 and 15 years old	153	3,322	4,334
16 and 17 years old	171	3,197	4,167
18 and 19 years old	124	2,980	3,840
20 and 21 years old	147	3,089	3,972
22 to 24 years old	296	4,719	6,118
25 to 29 years old	529	7,360	9,570
30 to 34 years old	626	7,736	10,028
35 to 44 years old	1,070	17,383	21,921
45 to 54 years old	908	17,259	21,222
55 years old and over	1,176	30,122	35,200

SOURCE: U.S. Bureau of the Census, Current Population Reports: School Enrollment, "(Table) 1. Enrollment Status of the Population 3 Years Old and Over, by Age, Sex, Race, Hispanic 1 Origin, Nativity, and Selected Educational Characteristics: October 2004"; published October, 2005.

NOTES: 'All Races' includes other races not shown separately. 'White' and 'Asian' as shown are equivalent to 'White Alone' and 'Asian Alone', respectively.

UNITS: Estimates of the civilian non-institutionalized population, 3-years old and over as of October 1, in thousands of persons.

Table 3.04 Nursery School and Kindergarten Enrollment of Children 3 - 5 Years Old, by Selected Characteristics of the Mother, 2004

	Asian	White	All Races
All children 3 and 4 years old enrolled in nursery school	153	3,131	4,198
mother employed part-time	18	679	813
mother employed full-time	71	1,172	1,660
mother unemployed	4	82	161
mother with 0-8 years of school	-	90	107
with mother high school graduate	15	729	985
with mother with bachelor's degree or more	96	1,159	1,394
All children 3 and 4 years old enrolled in kindergarten	17	245	353
mother employed part-time	1	33	36
mother employed full-time	7	100	132
mother unemployed	-	11	25
mother with 0-8 years of school	-	24	24
with mother high school graduate	8	51	81
with mother with bachelor's degree or more	9	59	79

continued on the next page

Table 3.04 continued

	Asian	White	All Races
All children 5 years old enrolled in nursery school	12	377	474
mother employed part-time	3	50	62
mother employed full-time	6	121	171
mother unemployed	-	22	27
mother with 0-8 years of school	-	14	16
with mother high school graduate	1	58	82
with mother with bachelor's degree or more	8	132	150
All children 5 years old enrolled in kindergarten	133	2,223	2,943
mother employed part-time	10	399	502
mother employed full-time	69	829	1,162
mother unemployed	-	73	116
mother with 0-8 years of school	7	116	140
with mother high school graduate	26	563	743
with mother with bachelor's degree or more	73	644	826

SOURCE: U.S. Bureau of the Census, Current Population Reports: School Enrollment, "(Table) 4. Nursery School and Kindergarten Enrollment of People 3 to 6 Years Old, by Control of School, Attendance Status, Mother's Labor Force Status and Education, Family Income, Race, and Hispanic Origin: October 2004"; released October, 2005.

NOTES: 'All Races' includes other races/ethnic groups not shown separately. Includes children enrolled in public and non-public nursery school and kindergarten programs. Excludes five year olds enrolled in elementary school. 'All children' includes children whose mothers' labor force status is unknown and children with no mother present in the household. 'White' and 'Asian' as shown equivalent to 'White Alone' and 'Asian Alone', respectively.

UNITS: Enrollment in thousands of children enrolled. – represents or rounds to zero.

Table 3.05 Enrollment in Public Elementary and Secondary Schools, by State, Fall, 2003

	Asian	White	All Races
United States	4.4%	58.7%	100.0%
Alabama	0.9%	59.9%	100.0%
Alaska	6.5	58.9	"
Arizona	2.2	49.2	"
Arkansas	1.1	69.9	"
California	11.3	32.9	"
Colorado	3.1	64.5	"
Connecticut	3.2	68.3	"
Delaware	2.6	57.3	"
District of Columbia	1.6	4.3	"
Florida	2.0	51.3	"
Georgia	2.5	52.1	"
Hawaii	72.4	20.2	"
Idaho	1.5	84.1	"
Illinois	3.6	57.4	"
Indiana	1.1	81.5	"
Iowa	1.8	88.2	"
Kansas	2.3	76.4	"
Kentucky	0.8	87.0	"
Louisiana	1.3	48.5	"
Maine	1.2	95.8	"
Maryland	4.9	50.4	"
Massachusetts	4.7	74.6	"
Michigan	2.2	72.7	"
Minnesota	5.4	80.2	"
Mississippi	0.7	47.3	"
Missouri	1.4	77.7	"
Montana	1.0	85.1	"

continued on the next page

Table 3.05 continued

	Asian	White	All Races
Nebraska	1.7	79.5	100.0%
Nevada	6.7	50.8	"
New Hampshire	1.7	94.2	"
New Jersey	7.0%	57.9%	"
New Mexico	1.2	32.8	"
New York	6.6	53.9	"
North Carolina	2.0	58.3	"
North Dakota	0.8	88.0	"
Ohio	1.3	79.4	"
Oklahoma	1.5	61.5	"
Oregon	4.4	76.6	"
Pennsylvania	2.3	76.3	"
Rhode Island	3.2	71.2	"
South Carolina	1.1	54.2	"
South Dakota	1.0	84.9	"
Tennessee	1.3	70.7	"
Texas	2.9	38.7	"
Utah	2.9	83.4	"
Vermont	1.5	95.9	"
Virginia	4.7	61.3	"
Washington	7.9	71.5	"
West Virginia	0.6	94.1	"
Wisconsin	3.4	78.8	"
Wyoming	1.0	86.0	"

SOURCE: U.S. Department of Education, National Center for Education Statistics, Digest of Education Statistics, 2005, "(Table 38) Percentage Distribution of Enrollment in Public Elementary and Secondary Schools, by race/ethnicity and state or jurisdiction: Fall 1993 and Fall 2003". ED 1.113\ (year)

NOTES: 'All Races' includes other races and ethnic groups not shown separately. 'White' excludes persons of Hispanic origin.

UNITS: Enrollment as a percent of total enrollment, 100.0%.

Table 3.06 Elementary and High School Students With at Least One Foreign-Born Parent, 2003

	Asian	White	Total
Total number of elementary and high school students	1,890	29,716	49,626
Percent of all students with at least one foreign-born parent:			
total	91.0%	7.2%	21.9%
foreign-born student	23.0	1.5	5.6
native student	68.0	5.7	16.3

SOURCE: U.S. Census Bureau, Statistical Abstract of the United States: 2006; p. 146, table 213.

NOTES: 'Asian' excludes Pacific Islanders. 'White' exludes Hispanic origin.

UNITS: Number in thousands.

Table 3.07 SAT (Scholastic Aptitude Test) Scores, 1986 - 2005

	Asian	White	All Races
1986-1987			
verbal score	479	518	499
math score	541	513	500
1990-1991			
verbal score	485	518	499
math score	548	513	500
1995-1996			
verbal score	496	526	505
math score	558	523	508
2000-2001			
verbal score	501	529	506
math score	566	531	514
2001-2002			
verbal score	501	527	504
math score	569	533	516
2002-2003			
verbal score	508	529	507
math score	575	534	519
2003-2004			
verbal score	507	528	508
math score	577	531	518
2004-2005			
verbal score	511	532	508
math score	580	536	520

SOURCE: U.S. Department of Education, Center for Education Statistics, Digest of Education Statistics 2005; "(Table 126) SAT Score Averages of College-Bound Seniors, by Race/Ethnicity: Selected Years, 1986-87 through 2004-05". ED 1.113: (year)

NOTES: 'All Races' includes other races and ethnic groups not shown separately.

UNITS: Average scores, (minimum score, 200; maximum score 800).

Table 3.08 Labor Force Status of 2004 High School Graduates and 2004-05 High School Dropouts, October 2005

	Asian	White	Total
2005 high school graduates			
total	22	1,256	1,529
employed	22	1,106	1,320
unemployed	na	149	209
not in labor force	58	891	1,146
2004-05 high school dropouts			
total	6	166	233
employed	6	114	156
unemployed	1	52	77
not in labor force	na	106	174

SOURCE: U.S. Department Labor, Bureau of Labor Statistics, "(Table) 1. Labor force status of 2005 high school graduates and 2004-05 high school dropouts 16 to 24 years old by school enrollment, sex, race, and Hispanic origin, October 2005"; <http://stats.bls.gov/news.release/hsgec.t01.htm>.

NOTES: 'High school dropouts' refers to persons who dropped out of school between October 2004 and October 2005.

UNITS: Number of persons in thousands of persons.

Chapter 4: Education - Postsecondary & Educational Attainment

Table 4.01 College Enrollment, October 2004

	Asian	White	All Races
2004			
total enrolled	1,191	13,381	17,338
year enrolled in college			
1st year	209	3,118	4,150
2nd year	217	2,958	3,807
3rd year	152	2,637	3,291
4th year	205	2,114	2,757
5th year	150	1,006	1,324
6th year or higher	258	1,548	2,054

SOURCE: U.S. Bureau of the Census, Current Population Reports: School Enrollment, 2004; "(Table) 10. Type of College and Year Enrolled for College Students 15 Years Old and Over, by Age, Sex, Attendance Status, Race and Hispanic Origin: October 2004"; released October, 2005.

NOTES: 'All Races' includes other races and ethnic groups not shown separately. College enrollment at the undergraduate level in two and four year institutions. 'White' and 'Asian' as shown are equivalent to 'White Alone' and 'Asian Alone', respectively.

UNITS: College enrollment in thousands of students.

Table 4.02 School Enrollment by Attendance Status, Type and Control of School, Fall, 2004

	Asian	White	All Races
Total enrolled			
two-year college			
full time	146	1,966	2,602
part time	73	1,337	1,738
four-year college			
full time	472	6,170	7,816
part time	91	1,354	1,848
graduate college			
full time	263	1,120	1,571
part time	146	1,434	1,807
Total public			
two-year college			
full time	135	1,787	2,344
part time	67	1,220	1,596
four-year college			
full time	387	4,620	5,938
part time	73	1,127	1,507
graduate college			
full time	165	750	1,036
part time	101	973	1,231
Total private			
two-year college			
full time	10	179	258
part time	6	118	142
four-year college			
full time	86	1,551	1,878
part time	18	226	342
graduate college			
full time	98	370	536
part time	45	460	575

SOURCE: U.S. Bureau of the Census, Current Population Reports: School Enrollment, 2004; "(Table) 9. Enrollment of the Population 15 Years Old and Over, by School Type, Attendance Status, Control of School, Age, Sex, Race and Hispanic Origin: October 2004"; released October, 2005.

NOTES: 'All Races' includes other races not shown separately. 'White' and 'Asian' as shown are equivalent to 'White Alone' and 'Asian Alone', respectively.

UNITS: Enrollment in thousands of students.

Table 4.03 Enrollment in Institutions of Higher Education, by Type of Institution, 1980 - 2004

	Asian	White	All Races
1980			
All institutions	286.4	9,883.0	12,086.8
4-year institutions	162.1	6,274.5	7,565.4
2-year institutions	124.3	3,558.5	4,521.4
1990			
All institutions	572.4	10,722.5	13,818.6
4-year institutions	357.2	6,768.1	8,578.6
2-year institutions	215.2	3,954.3	5,240.1
1995			
All institutions	na	10,311.2	14,261.8
4-year institutions	na	6,517.2	8,769.3
2-year institutions	na	3,794.0	5,492.5
2000			
All institutions	978.2	10,462.1	15,312.3
4-year institutions	576.3	6,658.0	9,363.9
2-year institutions	401.9	3,804.1	5,948.4
2004			
All institutions	1,108.7	11,422.8	17,272.0
4-year institutions	678.0	7,359.0	10,726.2
2-year institutions	430.7	4,063.8	6,545.9

SOURCE: U.S. Department of Education, Center for Education Statistics, Digest of Education Statistics, 2005, "(Table 206) Total Fall Enrollment in Degree-Granting Institutions, by Race/Ethnicity of Student, Type, and Control of Institution". ED 1.113: (year)

NOTES: 'All Races' includes other races and ethnic groups not shown separately. 'White' excludes persons of Hispanic origin.

UNITS: Enrollment in thousands of students enrolled.

Table 4.04 Enrollment in Institutions of Higher Education, by State, Fall, 2004

	Asian	White	All Races
UNITED STATES	1,108,693	11,422,770	17,272,044
Alabama	3,342	166,656	255,826
Alaska	1,344	22,316	30,869
Arizona	17,588	315,925	490,925
Arkansas	1,996	104,737	138,399
California	444,352	1,040,123	2,374,045
Colorado	11,490	231,068	300,914
Connecticut	7,440	126,513	172,775
Delaware	1,371	35,935	49,804
District of Columbia	6,627	48,634	99,988
Florida	29,044	492,832	866,665
Georgia	15,616	262,308	434,283
Hawaii	40,412	17,952	67,225
Idaho	1,397	67,429	76,311
Illinois	47,237	524,866	801,401
Indiana	7,115	295,973	356,801
Iowa	4,466	189,641	217,646
Kansas	6,737	156,552	191,590
Kentucky	2,799	208,553	240,097
Louisiana	5,037	150,456	246,301
Maine	1,013	60,277	65,415
Maryland	19,868	182,062	312,493
Massachusetts	31,650	319,010	439,245
Michigan	20,515	475,409	620,980
Minnesota	14,877	292,323	349,021
Mississippi	1,254	88,612	152,115
Missouri	8,993	290,291	365,204
Montana	503	40,219	47,173
Nebraska	2,790	104,754	121,053
Nevada	10,777	69,004	105,961
New Hampshire	1,784	63,040	70,163

continued on the next page

Table 4.04 continued

	Asian	White	All Races
New Jersey	32,232	228,670	380,374
New Mexico	2,527	57,086	131,577
New York	88,274	698,133	1,141,525
North Carolina	11,252	320,135	472,709
North Dakota	488	42,560	49,533
Ohio	12,994	497,895	614,234
Oklahoma	4,674	146,224	207,625
Oregon	12,606	163,889	199,985
Pennsylvania	28,457	546,202	688,780
Rhode Island	3,420	64,546	80,377
South Carolina	3,088	140,288	208,910
South Dakota	396	42,049	48,708
Tennessee	5,143	207,872	278,055
Texas	60,221	645,856	1,229,197
Utah	5,643	170,333	194,324
Vermont	828	35,301	38,639
Virginia	23,322	293,131	425,181
Washington	32,297	262,771	343,524
West Virginia	1,072	88,168	97,884
Wisconsin	9,191	285,736	331,506
Wyoming	298	30,700	33,955

SOURCE: U.S. Department of Education, Center for Education Statistics, Digest of Education Statistics, 2005; "(Table 208) Fall Enrollment in Degree-Granting Institutions, by Race/Ethnicity of Student and by State or Jurisdiction: 2004"; prepared September 2005. ED 1.113: (year)

NOTES: 'All Races' includes other races and ethnic groups not shown separately. 'White' excludes Hispanic. 'Asian' as shown is equivalent to 'Asian and Pacific Islander'.

UNITS: Enrollment in number of students enrolled.

Table 4.05 Enrollment in Schools of Medicine, Dentistry and Related Fields, 1980-81 and 2002-2003

	Asian	White	All Races
1980-81			
allopathic medicine	3.0%	85.0%	100.0%
osteopathic medicine	1.8	94.9	"
podiatry	2.7	91.3	"
dentistry	4.6	88.5	"
optometry	5.2	91.4	"
pharmacy	4.8	88.6	"
2002-2003			
dentistry	6.0%	63.7%	100.0%
allopathic medicine	6.4	64.0	"
osteopathic medicine	3.7	73.6	"
registered nursing	na	na	"
optometry	5.6	60.3	"
pharmacy	3.8	58.5	"
podiatry	7.3	60.7	"

SOURCE: U.S. Department of Health and Human Services, Health United States, 2005; pp. 348-349, table 110.

NOTES: 'All Races' includes other races and ethnic groups not shown separately. 'White' excludes Hispanic persons. 'Asian' includes Asian or Pacific Islander.

UNITS: Enrollment as a percentage of all students enrolled, 100.0%.

Table 4.06 Undergraduates Receiving Financial Aid: Average Amount Awarded per Student, by Type and Source of Aid, 2003-2004

	Asian	White	All Races
2003-2004			
All full-time, full-year enrolled undergraduates	1,127	12,025	19,054
undergraduates receiving:			
any aid, total	$10,039	$9,919	$9,899
- from federal source	6,745	7,318	7,304
- from non-federal sources	6,180	5,733	5,586
grants, total	$6,700	$5,479	$5,565
- from federal source	3,411	3,075	3,247
- from non-federal sources	5,545	4,887	4,828
loans, total	$7,079	$7,443	$7,336
- from federal source	6,136	6,450	6,426
- from non-federal sources	6,728	6,222	6,089
work-study funds, total	$2,027	$1,917	$1,942

SOURCE: U.S. Department of Education, Center for Education Statistics, Digest of Education Statistics, 2005; "(Table 317) Average Amount of Financial Aid Awarded to Full-Time, Full-Year Undergraduates, by Type and Source of Aid and Selected Student Characteristics: 2003-04"; "(Table 316) Percentage of Undergraduates Receiving Aid, by Type and Source of Aid and Selected Student Characteristics: 2003-04." ED 1.113\(year)

NOTES: 'All Races' includes other races and ethnic groups not shown separately. 'White' excludes Hispanic persons.

UNITS: Number of undergraduates, in thousands.

Table 4.07 Educational Attainment, 2003

	Asian	White	Total
Population	7,691	133,488	185,183
percent:			
High school graduate or more	87.6%	89.4%	84.6%
Some college or more	67.4	56.4	52.5
Bachelor's degree or more	49.8	30.0	27.2

SOURCE: U.S. Census Bureau, Current Population Survey, Annual Social and Economic Supplement, 2003.

NOTES: 'White' excludes Hispanics. 'Asian' refers to people who reported a single race of Asian.

UNITS: Population 25 years or older, in thousands.

Table 4.08 Earned Degrees Conferred, by Type of Degree, 2001 - 2004

	Asian	White	All Races
2001-2002			
Associate's degree	30,947	417,739	595,133
Bachelor's degrees	83,101	958,585	1,291,900
Master's degrees	25,414	327,635	482,118
Doctor's degrees	2,317	26,905	44,160
First Professional degrees	9,584	58,874	80,698
2003-2004			
Associate's degree	33,149	456,047	665,301
Bachelor's degrees	92,073	1,026,114	1,399,542
Master's degrees	30,952	369,582	558,940
Doctor's degrees	2,632	28,214	48,378
First Professional degrees	9,964	60,379	83,041

SOURCE: U.S. Department of Education, Center for Education Statistics, Digest of Education Statistics, 2003; p. 335, table 265; p. 338, table 268; p. 341, table 271; p. 344, table 274; 2005; table 259, table 262 table 265, table 268, table 271. ED 1.113\(year)

NOTES: 'All Races' includes other races and ethnic groups not shown separately. 'White' excludes Hispanic persons. 'First professional Degrees' include degrees awarded in chiropractic, dentistry, law, medicine, optometry, osteopathy, pharmacy, podiatry, theology, and veterinary medicine.

UNITS: Earned degrees conferred in number of degrees.

Table 4.09 Associate Degrees Conferred, by Major Field of Study, 2003-2004

	Asian	White	All Races
All Fields, Total	33,149	456,047	665,301
agriculture and natural resources	45	5,887	6,283
architecture and related programs	12	330	492
area, ethnic and cultural studies	2	20	105
biological sciences/life sciences	147	912	1,456
business	5,963	68,615	106,304
communications & journalism	81	1,779	2,444
communications technologies	124	2,506	3,401
computer and information sciences	2,666	27,160	41,845
construction trades	70	3,095	3,560
education	199	7,931	12,465
engineering	175	1,573	2,737
engineering technologies	1,848	26,158	36,915
English language and literature/letters	52	531	828
family & consumer sciences	330	4,991	9,478
foreign languages and literatures	24	723	1,047
health professions and related sciences	3,771	78,649	106,208
legal professions & studies	161	6,410	9,466
liberal arts/general studies/humanities	12,650	154,929	227,650
library science	7	97	114
mathematics & statistics	106	461	801
mechanics and repairers	607	9,705	12,553
military technologies	9	176	293
multi/interdisciplinary studies	1,311	9,863	14,794
parks, recreation, and fitness studies	21	717	923
philosophy and religion	18	335	404
physical sciences	244	1,817	2,676
precision production	45	1,733	1,968
psychology	80	1,206	1,887
public administration & social services	112	1,957	3,728
security & protective services	484	14,784	20,573
social sciences and history	429	3,580	6,245
theological studies/religious vocations	8	338	492
transportation	45	921	1,217
visual and performing arts	1,303	16,158	23,949

SOURCE: U.S. Department of Education, National Center for Education Statistics, Digest of Education Statistics, 2005; "(Table 259) Associate's Degrees Conferred by Degree-Granting Institutions, by Sex, Racial/Ethnicity Group, and Major Field of Study: 2003-04"; prepared July 2005. ED 1.113\(year)

NOTES: 'All Races' includes other races and ethnic groups not shown separately. 'White' excludes Hispanic persons.

UNITS: Earned Associate degrees conferred in number of degrees.

Table 4.10 Bachelor's Degrees Conferred, by Major Field of Study, 2003- 2004

	Asian	White	All Races
All Fields, Total	92,073	1,026,114	1,399,542
agriculture and natural resources	653	20,216	22,835
architecture and related programs	698	6,604	8,838
area, ethnic and cultural studies	873	4,143	7,181
biological sciences/life sciences	7,838	42,926	61,509
business	22,185	213,892	307,149
communications & journalism	2,866	55,423	70,968
communications technologies	110	1,547	2,034
computer and information sciences	8,496	34,836	59,488
construction trades	1	103	119
education	1,759	91,279	106,278
engineering	8,046	43,615	63,558
engineering technologies	732	10,444	14,391
English language and literature/letters	2,175	43,656	53,984
family & consumer sciences	775	15,066	19,172
foreign languages and literatures	935	12,692	17,754
health professions and related sciences	3,758	56,033	73,934
legal professions & studies	182	1,931	2,841
liberal arts/general studies/humanities	1,875	29,164	42,106
library science	0	69	72
mathematics & statistics	1,283	9,861	13,327
mechanics and repairers	3	131	159
military technologies	0	10	10
multi/interdisciplinary studies	2,047	20,743	29,162
parks, recreation, and fitness studies	569	17,621	22,164
philosophy and religion	574	9,234	11,152
physical sciences	1,384	13,973	17,983
precision production	1	58	61
psychology	4,555	59,480	82,098
public administration & social services	642	12,845	20,552
security & protective services	731	18,964	28,175
social sciences and history	11,197	108,775	150,357
theological studies/religious vocations	182	6,882	8,126
transportation	153	3,995	4,824
visual and performing arts	4,795	59,903	77,181

SOURCE: U.S. Department of Education, National Center for Education Statistics, Digest of Education Statistics, 2005; "(Table 262) Bachelor's Degrees Conferred by Degree-Granting Institutions, by Sex, Racial/Ethnicity Group, and Major Field of Study: 2003-04"; prepared July 2005. ED 1.113\(year)

NOTES: 'All Races' includes other races and ethnic groups not shown separately. 'White' excludes Hispanic persons.

UNITS: Earned Bachelor's degrees conferred in number of degrees.

Table 4.11 Master's Degrees Conferred, by Major Field of Study, 2003-2004

	Asian	White	All Races
All Fields, Total	30,952	369,582	558,940
agriculture and natural resources	135	3,516	4,783
architecture and related programs	301	3,330	5,424
area, ethnic and cultural studies	112	998	1,683
biological sciences/life sciences	835	4,907	7,657
business	10,488	85,082	139,347
communications & journalism	315	4,162	6,535
communications technologies	37	177	365
computer and information sciences	2,760	6,696	20,143
construction trades	0	0	0
education	3,967	126,634	163,345
engineering	3,151	12,131	32,698
engineering technologies	217	1,385	2,499
English language and literature/letters	267	6,491	7,956
family & consumer sciences	53	1,281	1,794
foreign languages and literatures	123	1,783	3,124
health professions and related sciences	3,269	32,735	44,939
legal professions & studies	243	1,414	4,243
liberal arts/general studies/humanities	89	2,988	3,697
library science	174	5,011	6,015
mathematics & statistics	295	1,937	4,191
mechanics and repairers	0	0	0
military technologies	0	0	0
multi/interdisciplinary studies	186	2,741	4,047
parks, recreation, and fitness studies	88	2,503	3,199
philosophy and religion	73	1,222	1,578
physical sciences	249	3,397	5,570
precision production	0	10	13
psychology	715	12,951	17,898
public administration & social services	1,037	18,183	28,250
security & protective services	86	2,672	3,717
social sciences and history	720	9,903	16,110
theological studies/religious vocations	265	3,973	5,486
transportation	22	589	728
visual and performing arts	680	8,780	12,906

SOURCE: U.S. Department of Education, National Center for Education Statistics, Digest of Education Statistics, 2005; "(Table 265) Master's Degrees Conferred by Degree-Granting Institutions, by Sex, Racial/Ethnicity Group, and Major Field of Study: 2003-04"; prepared July 2005. ED 1.113\(year)

NOTES: 'All Races' includes other races and ethnic groups not shown separately. 'White' excludes Hispanic persons.

UNITS: Earned Master's degrees conferred in number of degrees.

Table 4.12 Doctor's Degrees Conferred, by Major Field of Study, 2003-2004

	Asian	White	All Races
All Fields, Total	2,632	28,214	48,378
agriculture and natural resources	33	587	1,185
architecture and related programs	13	69	173
area, ethnic and cultural studies	20	109	209
biological sciences/life sciences	496	3,072	5,242
business	67	673	1,481
communications & journalism	19	250	418
communications technologies	0	5	8
computer and information sciences	69	344	909
construction trades	0	0	0
education	203	4,746	7,088
engineering	368	1,751	5,923
engineering technologies	4	20	58
English language and literature/letters	49	939	1,207
family & consumer sciences	7	198	329
foreign languages and literatures	39	567	1,031
health professions and related sciences	286	3,144	4,361
legal professions & studies	3	17	119
liberal arts/general studies/humanities	1	76	95
library science	3	24	47
mathematics & statistics	50	419	1,060
mechanics and repairers	0	0	0
military technologies	0	0	0
multi/interdisciplinary studies	61	575	876
parks, recreation, and fitness studies	9	146	222
philosophy and religion	26	454	595
physical sciences	192	1,929	3,815
precision production	0	0	0
psychology	247	3,684	4,827
public administration & social services	23	407	649
security & protective services	0	46	54
social sciences and history	152	2,354	3,811
theological studies/religious vocations	116	762	1,304
transportation	0	0	0
visual and performing arts	76	847	1,282

SOURCE: U.S. Department of Education, National Center for Education Statistics, Digest of Education Statistics, 2005; "(Table 268) Doctor's Degrees Conferred by Degree-Granting Institutions, by Sex, Racial/Ethnicity Group, and Major Field of Study: 2003-04"; prepared July 2005. ED 1.113\(year)

NOTES: 'All Races' includes other races and ethnic groups not shown separately. 'White' excludes Hispanic persons.

UNITS: Earned Doctor's degrees conferred in number of degrees.

Table 4.13 First Professional Degrees Conferred, by Field of Study, 2003-2004

	Asian	White	All Races
All Fields, Total	9,964	60,379	83,041
Dentistry	896	2,703	4,335
Medicine	3,034	10,255	15,442
Optometry	326	815	1,275
Osteopathic medicine	447	2,064	2,722
Pharmacy	1,910	5,076	8,221
Podiatry	52	237	382
Veterinary medicine	60	2,003	2,228
Chiropractic medicine	211	2,129	2,730
Naturopathic medicine	9	141	165
Law	2,768	31,087	40,209
Theological professions	251	3,869	5,332

SOURCE: U.S. Department of Education, National Center for Education Statistics, Digest of Education Statistics, 2005; "(Table 271) First-Professional Degrees Conferred by Degree-Granting Institutions, by Sex, Racial/Ethnicity Group, and Major Field of Study: 2003-04". ED 1.113\(year)

NOTES: 'All Races' includes other races and ethnic groups not shown separately. 'White' excludes Hispanic persons.

UNITS: Earned first professional degrees conferred, in number of degrees.

Chapter 5: Government & Elections

Table 5.01 Members of Congress, 1985 - 2003

	Asian	White	All Races
House of Representatives			
99th Congress, 1985	5	412	435
100th Congress, 1987	6	408	433
101st Congress, 1989	6	406	435
102nd Congress, 1991	5	407	"
103rd Congress, 1993	7	393	"
104th Congress, 1995	7	391	"
106th Congress, 1999	6	na	"
107th Congress, 2001	7	na	443
108th Congress, 2003	5	na	435
Senate			
99th Congress, 1985	2	98	100
100th Congress, 1987	2	98	"
101st Congress, 1989	3	98	"
102nd Congress, 1991	2	98	"
103rd Congress, 1993	2	97	"
104th Congress, 1995	2	97	"
106th Congress, 1999	2	na	"
107th Congress, 2001	2	na	"
108th Congress, 2003	2	na	"

SOURCE: U.S. Bureau of the Census, Statistical Abstract of the United States, 2006; p. 257, table 395.

NOTES: 'Asian" includes Asian and Pacific Islanders. 'All Races' includes other races and ethnic groups not shown separately.

UNITS: Number of members of the House and Senate respectively, as shown.

Table 5.02 Voting Age Population, Registration, and Voting, 1990 - 2004

	Asian	White	All Races
Voting age population			
1990	na	155.6	182.1
1992	na	157.8	185.7
1994	na	160.3	190.3
1996	na	162.8	193.7
1998	7.3	165.8	198.2
2000	8.0	168.8	202.6
2002	9.6	174.1	210.4
2004*	9.3	176.6	215.7
Presidential election years			
percent reporting registration			
1992	31.2	70.1	68.2
1996	32.6	67.7	65.9
2000	30.7	70.4	63.9
2004*	34.9	67.9	65.9
percent reporting voting			
1992	27.3	63.6	61.3
1996	25.7	56.0	54.2
2000	25.4	60.5	54.7
2004*	29.8	60.3	58.3

continued on the next page

Table 5.02 continued

	Asian	White	All Races
Congressional election years (non-presidential election years)			
percent reporting registration			
1990	28.4%	63.8%	62.2%
1994	28.7	64.6	62.5
1998	29.1	63.9	62.1
2002	30.7	63.1	60.9
percent reporting voting			
1990	20.3%	46.7%	45.0%
1994	21.8	47.3	45.0
1998	19.3	43.3	41.9
2002	19.4	44.1	42.3

SOURCE: U.S. Bureau of the Census, Historical Time Series Tables; published May 2005; "(Table A-4) Reported Voting and Registration for Total and Citizen Voting-Age Population: Congressional Elections 1982-2002"; "(Table A-6) Reported Voting and Registration for Total and Citizen Voting-Age Population: Presidential Elections 1980-2004".
U.S. Bureau of the Census, Current Population Reports: Voting and Registration in the Election of November, 1998; "(Table 2). Reported Voting and Registration, by Race, Hispanic Origin, Sex, and Age, for the United States: November 1998"; published July 2000; 2000; published February 2002; 2002; published July 2004; 2004; published May 2005.

NOTES: 'All Races' includes other races and ethnic groups not shown separately. '*' denotes year(s) in which 'Asian' and 'White' as shown are equivalent to 'Asian Alone' and 'White Alone' respectively. Otherwise, 'Asian' is equivalent to 'Non-Hispanic Asian and Pacific Islander'.

UNITS: Voting age population in millions of persons; percent reporting registration and percent reporting voting as a percent of the voting age population.

Table 5.03 Voting Age Population, Selected Characteristics, 1998

	Asian	White	All Races
Voting age population, 1998			
by age			
total 18 years and over	7,327	165,821	198,228
18-24 years old	1,058	20,508	25,537
25-44 years old	3,562	67,686	82,993
45-64 years old	1,974	48,955	57,436
65-74 years old	461	15,688	17,902
75 years and over	273	12,984	14,361
by sex			
male	3,477	80,450	95,187
female	3,851	85,371	103,042
by years of school completed			
less than 9th grade	560	11,078	13,338
9th to 12th grade, no diploma	452	16,433	21,017
high school graduate	1,610	55,084	65,579
some college or associate degree	1,772	44,228	52,903
bachelor's degree	1,926	26,157	30,475
advanced degree	1,007	12,840	14,916
by employment status			
in civilian labor force	5,003	113,485	135,726
unemployed	169	3,726	5,227

continued on the next page

Table 5.03 continued

	Asian	White	All Races
by family income			
under $5,000	137	1,742	2,866
$5,000-$9,999	161	3,493	5,149
$10,000-$14,999	217	6,536	8,446
$15,000-$24,999	658	13,504	16,790
$25,000-$34,999	626	16,008	19,347
$35,000-$49,999	898	21,060	24,576
$50,000-$74,999	1,156	25,365	28,988
$75,000 and over	1,376	26,577	29,582
income not reported	641	12,933	15,463

SOURCE: U.S. Bureau of the Census, Current Population Reports: Voting and Registration in the Election of November, 1998, "(Table 2). Reported Voting and Registration, by Race, Hispanic Origin, Sex, and Age, for the United States: November 1998"; "(Table 6). Reported Voting and Registration, by Race, Hispanic Origin, Sex, and Educational Attainment: November 1998"; "(Table 7). Reported Voting and Registration, by Race, Hispanic Origin, Sex, Employment Status and Class of Worker: November 1998"; " (Table 9). Reported Voting and Registration of Family Members, by Race, Hispanic Origin, and Family Income: November 1998;" published July 19, 2000.

NOTES: 'All Races' includes other races and ethnic groups not shown separately. 'Asian' as shown is equivalent to 'Non-Hispanic Asian and Pacific Islander'.

UNITS: Voting age population in thousands of persons.

Table 5.04 Selected Characteristics of Persons Registered to Vote, 1998

	Asian	White	All Races
Persons registered to vote, 1998			
by age			
total 18 years and over	29.1%	63.9%	62.1%
18-24 years old	18.0	40.7	39.2
25-44 years old	23.1	59.4	57.7
45-64 years old	40.2	72.6	71.1
65-74 years old	46.1	78.3	77.1
75 years and over	41.0	74.1	73.2
by sex			
male	28.5	62.5	60.6
female	29.6	65.2	63.5
by years of school completed			
less than 9th grade	11.9	39.5	40.2
9th to 12th grade, no diploma	12.0	43.3	43.4
high school graduate	27.0	60.0	58.6
some college or associate degree	29.9	70.0	68.3
bachelor's degree	33.9	76.7	73.8
advanced degree	39.2	80.9	77.7
by employment status			
in civilian labor force	31.7	63.6	62.1
unemployed	24.6	48.1	48.5

continued on the next page

Table 5.04 continued

	Asian	White	All Races
by family income			
under $5,000	7.1	40.9	41.5
$5,000-$9,999	10.6	42.0	44.9
$10,000-$14,999	17.9	48.2	49.0
$15,000-$24,999	15.3	55.1	54.2
$25,000-$34,999	32.2	61.2	60.6
$35,000-$49,999	27.7	67.7	65.7
$50,000-$74,999	29.5	73.8	71.9
$75,000 and over	49.3	78.9	77.3
income not reported	18.8	55.1	52.1

SOURCE: U.S. Bureau of the Census, Current Population Reports: Voting and Registration in the Election of November, 1998, "(Table 2). Reported Voting and Registration, by Race, Hispanic Origin, Sex, and Age, for the United States: November 1998"; "(Table 6). Reported Voting and Registration, by Race, Hispanic Origin, Sex, and Educational Attainment: November 1998"; "(Table 7). Reported Voting and Registration, by Race, Hispanic Origin, Sex, Employment Status and Class of Worker: November 1998"; " (Table 9). Reported Voting and Registration of Family Members, by Race, Hispanic Origin, and Family Income: November 1998;" published July 19, 2000.

NOTES: 'All Races' includes other races and ethnic groups not shown separately. 'Asian' as shown is equivalent to 'Non-Hispanic Asian and Pacific Islander'.

UNITS: Person reporting registration to vote as a percent of the voting age population, 100.0%.

Table 5.05 Selected Characteristics of Persons Voting, 1998

	Asian	White	All Races
Persons voting, 1990			
by age			
total 18 years and over	19.2%	43.3%	41.9%
18-24 years old	9.8	17.2	16.6
25-44 years old	12.9	35.8	34.8
45-64 years old	29.5	54.7	53.6
65-74 years old	38.6	64.5	63.3
75 years and over	30.1	55.6	54.8
by sex			
male	18.6	43.0	41.4
female	19.7	43.7	42.4
by years of school completed			
less than 9th grade	7.7	23.1	24.0
9th to 12th grade, no diploma	8.6	24.5	24.6
high school graduate	17.4	38.1	37.1
some college or associate degree	20.9	47.5	46.2
bachelor's degree	21.0	56.2	54.0
advanced degree	26.6	66.8	63.6
by employment status			
in civilian labor force	20.4	41.8	40.7
unemployed	19.9	28.7	28.4

continued on the next page

Table 5.05 continued

	Asian	White	All Races
by family income			
under $5,000	4.7	21.3	21.1
$5,000-$9,999	10.0	22.3	23.9
$10,000-$14,999	11.4	30.9	30.4
$15,000-$24,999	9.0	35.7	34.6
$25,000-$34,999	22.1	40.5	40.2
$35,000-$49,999	18.1	45.3	44.0
$50,000-$74,999	17.9	51.2	49.9
$75,000 and over	33.9	58.4	57.3
income not reported	14.6	40.0	37.8

SOURCE: U.S. Bureau of the Census, Current Population Reports: Voting and Registration in the Election of November, 1998, "(Table 2). Reported Voting and Registration, by Race, Hispanic Origin, Sex, and Age, for the United States: November 1998"; "(Table 6). Reported Voting and Registration, by Race, Hispanic Origin, Sex, and Educational Attainment: November 1998"; "(Table 7). Reported Voting and Registration, by Race, Hispanic Origin, Sex, Employment Status and Class of Worker: November 1998"; " (Table 9). Reported Voting and Registration of Family Members, by Race, Hispanic Origin, and Family Income: November 1998;" published July 19, 2000.

NOTES: 'All Races' includes other races and ethnic groups not shown separately. 'Asian' as shown is equivalent to 'Non-Hispanic Asian and Pacific Islander'.

UNITS: Persons reporting voting as a percent of the voting age population, 100.0%.

Table 5.06 Voting Age Population, Selected Characteristics, 2000

	Asian	White	All Races
Voting age population, 2000			
Total, 18 years and over	8,041	168,733	202,609
by sex			
male	3,767	69,290	97,087
female	4,274	74,361	105,523
by age			
18-24 years old	1,237	21,295	26,712
25-44 years old	3,818	66,378	81,780
45-64 years old	2,187	52,038	61,352
65-74 years old	472	15,493	17,819
75 years and over	327	13,529	14,945
by educational attainment			
less than 9th grade	622	10,626	12,894
9th to 12th grade, no diploma	460	15,822	20,108
high school graduate or GED	1,789	55,530	66,339
some college or associate degree	1,865	45,923	55,308
bachelor's degree	2,208	27,382	32,254
advanced degree	1,097	13,450	15,706
by employment status			
in civilian labor force	5,594	115,103	138,378
unemployed	183	3,544	4,944

continued on the next page

Table 5.06 continued

	Asian	White	All Races
by family income			
less than $5,000	112	1,405	2,230
$5,000-$9,999	149	2,732	4,242
$10,000-$14,999	224	5,390	7,286
$15,000-$24,999	526	11,568	14,600
$25,000-$34,999	682	14,578	17,692
$35,000-$49,999	788	18,907	22,349
$50,000-$74,999	1,061	24,250	28,144
$75,000 and over	1,971	31,021	35,030
income not reported	745	17,518	20,721

SOURCE: U.S. Bureau of the Census, Current Population Reports: Voting and Registration in the Election of November, 2000; published February 2002; "(Table 2). Reported Voting and Registration, by Race, Hispanic Origin, Sex, and Age, for the United States: November 2000"; "(Table 6). Reported Voting and Registration, by Race, Hispanic Origin, Sex, and Educational Attainment: November 2000"; "(Table 7). Reported Voting and Registration, by Race, Hispanic Origin, Sex, Employment Status and Class of Worker: November 2000"; " (Table 9). Reported Voting and Registration of Family Members, by Race, Hispanic Origin, and Family Income: November 2000".

NOTES: 'All Races' includes other races and ethnic groups not shown separately. 'Asian' as shown is equivalent to 'Asian and Pacific Islander'.

UNITS: Voting age population in thousands of persons.

Table 5.07 Selected Characteristics of Persons Registered to Vote, 2000

	Asian	White	All Races
Voting age population, 2000			
Total, 18 years and over	30.7%	65.6%	63.9%
by sex			
male	31.8	64.0	62.2
female	29.8	67.2	65.6
by age			
18-24 years old	22.2	46.3	45.4
25-44 years old	26.7	61.2	59.6
45-64 years old	38.1	72.7	71.2
65-74 years old	43.7	77.3	76.2
75 years and over	41.7	77.2	76.1
by educational attainment			
less than 9th grade	14.0	34.8	36.1
9th to 12th grade, no diploma	17.0	44.8	45.9
high school graduate or GED	28.2	61.3	60.1
some college or associate degree	32.1	71.8	70.0
bachelor's degree	36.7	79.6	76.3
advanced degree	35.8	83.1	79.4
by employment status			
in civilian labor force	32.2	65.5	64.0
unemployed	15.7	44.9	46.1

continued on the next page

Table 5.07 continued

	Asian	White	All Races
by family income			
less than $5,000	5.0	40.7%	44.0
$5,000-$9,999	22.1	45.3	48.8
$10,000-$14,999	21.7	47.5	49.8
$15,000-$24,999	21.8	55.1	54.9
$25,000-$34,999	27.2	61.9	61.0
$35,000-$49,999	31.8	68.8	67.1
$50,000-$74,999	33.5	75.9	73.8
$75,000 and over	40.6	80.7	78.4
income not reported	26.2	55.5	54.2

SOURCE: U.S. Bureau of the Census, Current Population Reports: Voting and Registration in the Election of November, 2000; published February 2002; "(Table 2). Reported Voting and Registration, by Race, Hispanic Origin, Sex, and Age, for the United States: November 2000"; "(Table 6). Reported Voting and Registration, by Race, Hispanic Origin, Sex, and Educational Attainment: November 2000"; "(Table 7). Reported Voting and Registration, by Race, Hispanic Origin, Sex, Employment Status and Class of Worker: November 2000"; " (Table 9). Reported Voting and Registration of Family Members, by Race, Hispanic Origin, and Family Income: November 2000".

NOTES: 'All Races' includes other races and ethnic groups not shown separately. 'Asian' as shown is equivalent to 'Asian and Pacific Islander'.

UNITS: Persons registered to vote as a percent of the voting age population, 100.0%..

Table 5.08 Selected Characteristics of Persons Voting, 2000

	Asian	White	All Races
Voting age population, 2000			
Total, 18 years and over	25.4%	47.4%	41.9%
by sex			
male	26.0	47.3	41.4
female	24.9	47.4	42.4
by age			
18-24 years old	15.9	33.0	32.3
25-44 years old	22.2	51.2	49.8
45-64 years old	32.0	65.6	64.1
65-74 years old	40.4	71.1	69.9
75 years and over	34.4	66.2	64.9
by educational attainment			
less than 9th grade	10.3	25.8	26.8
9th to 12th grade, no diploma	15.1	32.7	33.6
high school graduate or GED	21.7	50.4	49.4
some college or associate degree	25.2	62.0	60.3
bachelor's degree	32.0	73.4	70.3
advanced degree	31.5	79.3	75.5
by employment status			
in civilian labor force	26.8	56.2	54.8
unemployed	13.7	34.6	35.1

continued on the next page

Table 5.08 continued

	Asian	White	All Races
by family income			
less than $5,000	4.2%	27.3%	28.2%
$5,000-$9,999	20.8	32.5	34.7
$10,000-$14,999	17.1	35.6	37.7
$15,000-$24,999	14.3	43.3	43.4
$25,000-$34,999	24.6	51.8	51.0
$35,000-$49,999	24.3	58.8	57.5
$50,000-$74,999	26.2	67.1	65.2
$75,000 and over	34.8	73.8	71.5
income not reported	23.3	49.6	48.2

SOURCE: U.S. Bureau of the Census, Current Population Reports: Voting and Registration in the Election of November, 2000; published February 2002; "(Table 2). Reported Voting and Registration, by Race, Hispanic Origin, Sex, and Age, for the United States: November 2000"; "(Table 6). Reported Voting and Registration, by Race, Hispanic Origin, Sex, and Educational Attainment: November 2000"; "(Table 7). Reported Voting and Registration, by Race, Hispanic Origin, Sex, Employment Status and Class of Worker: November 2000"; " (Table 9). Reported Voting and Registration of Family Members, by Race, Hispanic Origin, and Family Income: November 2000".

NOTES: 'All Races' includes other races and ethnic groups not shown separately. 'Asian' as shown is equivalent to 'Asian and Pacific Islander'.

UNITS: Persons reporting voting as a percent of the voting age population, 100.0%.

Table 5.09 Voting Age Population, Selected Characteristics, 2002

	Asian	White	All Races
Voting age population, 2002			
Total, 18 years and over	9,631	174,099	210,421
by sex			
male	4,569	84,466	100,939
female	5,062	89,633	109,481
by age			
18-24 years old	1,368	21,728	27,377
25-44 years old	4,540	66,238	82,228
45-64 years old	2,803	56,204	66,924
65-74 years old	573	15,653	17,967
75 years and over	348	14,276	15,925
by educational attainment			
less than 9th grade	591	10,195	12,333
9th to 12th grade, no diploma	618	16,161	20,908
high school graduate or GED	2,011	57,210	68,866
some college or associate degree	2,272	47,538	57,343
bachelor's degree	2,666	28,693	34,095
advanced degree	1,472	14,302	16,877
by employment status			
in civilian labor force	6,660	118,094	142,635
unemployed	367	5,488	7,735

continued on the next page

Table 5.09 continued

	Asian	White	All Races
by family income			
less than $5,000	92	1,280	2,159
$5,000-$9,999	130	2,707	4,051
$10,000-$14,999	310	4,960	6,696
$15,000-$24,999	462	11,696	14,665
$25,000-$34,999	805	13,412	16,868
$35,000-$49,999	986	18,200	21,945
$50,000-$74,999	1,256	24,932	28,921
$75,000 and over	2,578	35,540	40,309
income not reported	1,107	18,188	22,278

SOURCE: U.S. Bureau of the Census, Current Population Reports: Voting and Registration in the Election of November, 2002; published July 2004; "(Table 2). Reported Voting and Registration, by Race, Hispanic Origin, Sex, and Age, for the United States: November 2002"; "(Table 6). Reported Voting and Registration, by Race, Hispanic Origin, Sex, and Educational Attainment: November 2002"; "(Table 7). Reported Voting and Registration, by Race, Hispanic Origin, Sex, Employment Status and Class of Worker: November 2002"; "(Table 9). Reported Voting and Registration of Family Members, by Race, Hispanic Origin, and Family Income: November 2002".

NOTES: 'All Races' includes other races not shown separately.

UNITS: Voting age population in thousands of persons.

Table 5.10 Selected Characteristics of Persons Registered to Vote, 2002

	Asian	White	All Races
Voting age population, 2002			
Total, 18 years and over	30.7%	63.1%	60.9%
by sex			
male	31.3	61.3	58.9
female	30.2	64.8	62.8
by age			
18-24 years old	21.7	39.2	38.2
25-44 years old	25.6	57.4	55.4
45-64 years old	41.1	71.3	69.4
65-74 years old	38.2	77.9	76.1
75 years and over	35.7	76.7	75.5
by educational attainment			
less than 9th grade	13.1	31.6	32.4
9th to 12th grade, no diploma	15.3	41.1	41.6
high school graduate or GED	25.1	58.7	57.1
some college or associate degree	33.9	68.8	66.7
bachelor's degree	36.9	76.7	73.3
advanced degree	35.7	81.3	76.6
by employment status			
in civilian labor force	33.5	62.8	60.9
Unemployed	24.0	48.6	48.1

continued on the next page

Table 5.10 continued

	Asian	White	All Races
by family income			
less than $5,000	17.5%	39.5%	45.2%
$5,000-$9,999	19.6	40.1	41.5
$10,000-$14,999	13.0	50.3	49.7
$15,000-$24,999	22.1	51.0	51.3
$25,000-$34,999	22.1	58.5	56.2
$35,000-$49,999	31.1	64.1	62.0
$50,000-$74,999	31.2	72.0	69.8
$75,000 and over	45.3	77.8	75.5
income not reported	20.3	54.4	52.0

SOURCE: U.S. Bureau of the Census, Current Population Reports: Voting and Registration in the Election of November, 2002; published July 2004; "(Table 2). Reported Voting and Registration, by Race, Hispanic Origin, Sex, and Age, for the United States: November 2002"; "(Table 6). Reported Voting and Registration, by Race, Hispanic Origin, Sex, and Educational Attainment: November 2002"; "(Table 7). Reported Voting and Registration, by Race, Hispanic Origin, Sex, Employment Status and Class of Worker: November 2002"; "(Table 9). Reported Voting and Registration of Family Members, by Race, Hispanic Origin, and Family Income: November 2002".

NOTES: 'All Races' includes other races not shown separately.

UNITS: Persons registered to vote as a percent of the voting age population, 100.0%.

Table 5.11 Selected Characteristics of Persons Voting, 2002

	Asian	White	All Races
Voting age population, 2002			
Total, 18 years and over	19.4%	44.1%	42.3%
by sex			
male	20.4	43.5	41.4
female	18.6	44.6	43.0
by age			
18-24 years old	10.0	17.4	17.2
25-44 years old	14.0	35.3	34.1
45-64 years old	29.7	54.8	53.1
65-74 years old	30.4	65.1	63.1
75 years and over	26.7	60.1	58.6
by educational attainment			
less than 9th grade	8.6	19.0	19.4
9th to 12th grade, no diploma	9.9	23.1	23.3
high school graduate or GED	15.8	38.3	37.1
some college or associate degree	20.7	47.3	45.8
bachelor's degree	23.4	59.1	56.2
advanced degree	23.6	67.7	63.2
by employment status			
in civilian labor force	21.3	42.7	41.3
unemployed	17.9	28.2	27.2

continued on the next page

Table 5.11 continued

	Asian	White	All Races
by family income			
less than $5,000	2.8%	19.6%	22.0%
$5,000-$9,999	5.6	19.8	20.7
$10,000-$14,999	7.4	31.1	30.5
$15,000-$24,999	14.1	31.9	32.0
$25,000-$34,999	13.1	40.2	38.3
$35,000-$49,999	20.0	44.2	42.7
$50,000-$74,999	19.9	51.7	50.1
$75,000 and over	31.9	58.3	56.6
income not reported	14.2	40.5	38.6

SOURCE: U.S. Bureau of the Census, Current Population Reports: Voting and Registration in the Election of November, 2002; published July 2004; "(Table 2). Reported Voting and Registration, by Race, Hispanic Origin, Sex, and Age, for the United States: November 2002"; "(Table 6). Reported Voting and Registration, by Race, Hispanic Origin, Sex, and Educational Attainment: November 2002"; "(Table 7). Reported Voting and Registration, by Race, Hispanic Origin, Sex, Employment Status and Class of Worker: November 2002"; "(Table 9). Reported Voting and Registration of Family Members, by Race, Hispanic Origin, and Family Income: November 2002".

NOTES: 'All Races' includes other races not shown separately.

UNITS: Persons reporting voting as a percent of the voting age population, 100.0%.

Table 5.12 Voting Age Population, Selected Characteristics, 2004

	Asian	White	All Races
Voting age population, 2004			
Total, 18 years and over	9,291	176,618	215,694
by sex			
male	4,406	85,984	103,812
female	4,885	90,634	111,882
by age			
18-24 years old	1,118	21,764	27,808
25-44 years old	4,318	65,317	82,133
45-64 years old	2,790	59,196	71,014
65-74 years old	600	15,783	18,363
75 years and over	464	14,557	16,375
by educational attainment			
less than 9th grade	635	10,431	12,574
9th to 12th grade, no diploma	507	15,793	20,719
high school graduate or GED	1,849	56,254	68,545
some college or associate degree	1,897	48,154	58,913
bachelor's degree	2,683	30,678	36,591
advanced degree	1,719	15,308	18,352
by employment status			
in civilian labor force	6,392	119,726	146,082
unemployed	263	5,030	7,251

continued on the next page

Table 5.12 continued

	Asian	White	All Races
by family income			
less than $10,000	207	4,088	6,404
$10,000-$14,999	198	4,874	6,565
$15,000-$19,999	207	4,386	5,859
$20,000-$29,999	497	12,339	15,574
$30,000-$39,999	724	14,042	17,194
$40,000-$49,999	470	11,170	13,281
$50,000-$74,999	1,284	25,568	30,179
$75,000-$99,999	881	15,707	18,123
$100,000-$149,999	933	12,894	14,905
$150,000 and over	641	8,003	9,120
income not reported	1,360	19,886	24,723

SOURCE: U.S. Bureau of the Census, Current Population Reports: Voting and Registration in the Election of November, 2004; published May 25, 2005;
"(Table 2). Reported Voting and Registration, by Race, Hispanic Origin, Sex, and Age, for the United States: November 2004";
"(Table 6). Reported Voting and Registration, by Race, Hispanic Origin, Sex, and Educational Attainment: November 2004";
"(Table 7). Reported Voting and Registration, by Race, Hispanic Origin, Sex, Employment Status and Class of Worker: November 2004";
"(Table 9). Reported Voting and Registration of Family Members, by Race, Hispanic Origin, and Family Income: November 2004".

NOTES: 'All Races' includes other races not shown separately. 'White' and 'Asian' as shown are equivalent to 'White Alone' and 'Asian Alone' respectively.

UNITS: Voting age population in thousands of persons.

Table 5.13 Selected Characteristics of Persons Registered to Vote, 2004

	Asian	White	All Races
Voting age population, 2004			
Total, 18 years and over	35.0%	67.9%	65.9%
by sex			
male	35.0	66.2	64.0
female	34.9	69.5	67.6
by age			
18-24 years old	29.1	52.5	51.5
25-44 years old	28.9	62.0	60.1
45-64 years old	43.4	74.6	72.7
65-74 years old	47.1	78.4	76.9
75 years and over	38.8	78.4	76.8
by educational attainment			
less than 9th grade	17.1	31.5	32.5
9th to 12th grade, no diploma	21.8	44.6	45.7
high school graduate or GED	32.4	62.7	61.5
some college or associate degree	38.9	75.6	73.7
bachelor's degree	38.8	80.9	77.0
advanced degree	37.7	85.5	80.3
by employment status			
in civilian labor force	37.0	68.5	66.5
Unemployed	36.8	55.2	56.3

continued on the next page

Table 5.13 continued

	Asian	White	All Races
by family income			
less than $10,000	26.2%	43.8%	49.5%
$10,000-$14,999	27.4	46.2	49.0
$15,000-$19,999	38.6	52.6	53.9
$20,000-$29,999	29.0	58.2	58.1
$30,000-$39,999	26.3	63.9	62.9
$40,000-$49,999	30.7	71.9	69.8
$50,000-$74,999	37.1	77.8	75.6
$75,000-$99,999	35.9	82.3	79.4
$100,000-$149,999	49.1	84.9	82.2
$150,000 and over	53.6	85.2	82.6
income not reported	30.3	56.1	53.0

SOURCE: U.S. Bureau of the Census, Current Population Reports: Voting and Registration in the Election of November, 2004; published May 25, 2005;
"(Table 2). Reported Voting and Registration, by Race, Hispanic Origin, Sex, and Age, for the United States: November 2004";
"(Table 6). Reported Voting and Registration, by Race, Hispanic Origin, Sex, and Educational Attainment: November 2004";
"(Table 7). Reported Voting and Registration, by Race, Hispanic Origin, Sex, Employment Status and Class of Worker: November 2004";
"(Table 9). Reported Voting and Registration of Family Members, by Race, Hispanic Origin, and Family Income: November 2004".

NOTES: 'All Races' includes other races not shown separately. 'White' and 'Asian' as shown are equivalent to 'White Alone' and 'Asian Alone' respectively.

UNITS: Persons registered to vote as a percent of the voting age population, 100.0%.

Table 5.14 Selected Characteristics of Persons Voting, 2004

	Asian	White	All Races
Voting age population, 2004			
Total, 18 years and over	29.8%	60.3%	58.3%
by sex			
male	29.0	58.6	56.3
female	30.5	62.0	60.1
by age			
18-24 years old	23.5	42.6	41.9
25-44 years old	23.9	54.0	52.2
45-64 years old	38.3	68.6	66.6
65-74 years old	43.7	72.4	70.8
75 years and over	31.1	68.4	66.7
by educational attainment			
less than 9th grade	12.5	22.7	23.6
9th to 12th grade, no diploma	16.0	33.3	34.6
high school graduate or GED	29.5	53.4	52.4
some college or associate degree	31.5	68.0	66.1
bachelor's degree	33.0	76.7	72.6
advanced degree	33.7	82.7	77.4
by employment status			
in civilian labor force	31.8	61.1	59.3
unemployed	31.7	45.1	46.4

continued on the next page

Table 5.14 continued

	Asian	White	All Races
by family income			
less than $10,000	21.3%	31.7%	36.5%
$10,000-$14,999	22.5	36.7	39.1
$15,000-$19,999	34.4	44.0	45.2
$20,000-$29,999	24.3	49.7	49.4
$30,000-$39,999	19.4	55.0	54.3
$40,000-$49,999	25.2	64.4	62.3
$50,000-$74,999	30.3	70.2	68.1
$75,000-$99,999	32.0	76.8	74.1
$100,000-$149,999	45.4	80.4	77.8
$150,000 and over	47.0	81.0	78.3
income not reported	26.5	50.4	47.6

SOURCE: U.S. Bureau of the Census, Current Population Reports: Voting and Registration in the Election of November, 2004; published May 25, 2005;
"(Table 2). Reported Voting and Registration, by Race, Hispanic Origin, Sex, and Age, for the United States: November 2004";
"(Table 6). Reported Voting and Registration, by Race, Hispanic Origin, Sex, and Educational Attainment: November 2004";
"(Table 7). Reported Voting and Registration, by Race, Hispanic Origin, Sex, Employment Status and Class of Worker: November 2004";
"(Table 9). Reported Voting and Registration of Family Members, by Race, Hispanic Origin, and Family Income: November 2004".

NOTES: 'All Races' includes other races not shown separately. 'White' and 'Asian' as shown are equivalent to 'White Alone' and 'Asian Alone' respectively.

UNITS: Persons reporting voting as a percent of the voting age population, 100.0%.

Table 5.15 Reasons for Not Registering, 2004

	Asian	White	All Races
Persons not registering to vote, 2004			
total 18 years and over	1,756	26,185	32,432
percent distribution			
not interested in the election or not involved in politics	37.7%	48.2%	46.6%
did not meet registration deadlines	14.4	17.5	17.4
not eligible to vote	13.1	6.0	6.7
don't know or refused	7.9	5.6	6.2
permanent illness or disability	4.3	5.5	5.6
did not know where or how to register	6.2	4.2	4.5
did not meet residency requirements	5.0	3.7	3.7
my vote would not make a difference	1.5	3.8	3.7
difficulty with English	6.2	0.8	1.0

SOURCE: U.S. Bureau of the Census, Current Population Reports: Voting and Registration in the Election of November, 2004; published May 25, 2005; "(Table E). Reasons for Not Registering by Selected Characteristics: 2004".

NOTES: 'All Races' includes other races and ethnic groups not shown separately. 'Asian' and 'White' as shown are equivalent to 'Asian Alone' and 'White Alone' respectively.

UNITS: Numbers in thousands. Percent distribution of reasons for not registering, 100.0%.

Table 5.16 Reasons for Not Voting, 2004

	Asian	White	All Races
Persons not voting, 2004			
total 18 years and over	479	13,341	16,334
percent distribution			
too busy, conflicting schedule	31.5%	19.4%	19.9%
illness or disability	6.1	15.6	15.4
other reason	13.7	10.9	10.9
not interested	7.9	10.8	10.7
did not like candidates or issues	4.4	10.6	9.9
out of town	11.6	9.4	9.0
don't know or refused	9.0	7.9	8.5
registration problems	6.1	6.8	6.8
forgot to vote	1.4	3.4	3.4
inconvenient polling place	5.5	3.0	3.0
transportation problems	1.3	1.9	2.1
bad weather conditions	1.5	0.4	0.5

SOURCE: U.S. Bureau of the Census, Current Population Reports: Voting and Registration in the Election of November, 2004; published May 25, 2005;
"(Table F). Reasons for Not Voting by Selected Characteristics: 2004".

NOTES: 'All Races' includes other races and ethnic groups not shown separately. 'Asian' and 'White' as shown are equivalent to 'Asian Alone' and 'White Alone' respectively.

UNITS: Numbers in thousands. Percent distribution of reasons for not voting, 100.0%.

Chapter 6: The Labor Force, Employment & Unemployment

Table 6.01 Labor Force Participation of the Civilian Noninstitutional Population 16 Years Old and Over, by Age, 2005

	Asian	White	All Races
2005			
civilian noninstitutional population			
all persons 16 years old and over	9,842	184,446	226,082
- persons 16-19 years old	616	12,690	16,398
- persons 65 years old and over	1,093	30,556	35,068
civilian labor force			
all persons 16 years old and over	6,503	122,299	149,320
- persons 16-19 years old	160	5,950	7,164
- persons 65 years old and over	170	4,624	5,278
labor force participation rate			
all persons 16 years old and over	66.1%	66.3%	66.0%
- persons 16-19 years old	26.0	46.9	43.7
- persons 65 years old and over	15.5	15.1	15.1

SOURCE: U.S. Department of Labor, Bureau of Labor Statistics, *Employment and Earnings*, 2006; pp. 205-208, table 3; p. 209, table 4 (data from the Current Population Survey). L2.41/2:(vol)/1:(year)

NOTES: 'All Races' includes other races and ethnic groups not shown separately.

UNITS: Civilian noninstitutional population and civilian labor force in thousands of persons; participation rate as a percent (the civilian noninstitutional population divided by the civilian labor force).

Table 6.02 Labor Force Participation of the Civilian Noninstitutional Population 16 Years Old and Over, by Sex and Age, 2005

	Asian		White		All Races	
	male	female	male	female	male	female
2005						
civilian noninstitutional population						
all persons 16 years old and over	4,679	5,163	90,027	94,419	109,151	116,931
- persons 16-19 years old	317	299	6,471	6,219	8,317	8,081
- persons 65 years old and over	474	619	13,123	17,433	14,944	20,125
civilian labor force						
all persons 16 years old and over	3,500	3,002	66,694	55,605	80,033	69,288
- persons 16-19 years old	81	79	2,988	2,962	3,590	3,574
- persons 65 years old and over	94	76	2,631	1,993	2,959	2,319
labor force participation rate						
all persons 16 years old and over	74.8%	58.2%	74.1%	58.9%	73.3%	59.3%
- persons 16-19 years old	25.6	26.5	46.2	47.6	43.2	44.2
- persons 65 years old and over	19.8	12.3	20.0	11.4	19.8	11.5

SOURCE: U.S. Department of Labor, Bureau of Labor Statistics, *Employment and Earnings*, 2006; pp. 205-208, table 3; p. 209, table 4 (data from the Current Population Survey). L2.41/2:(vol)/1:(year)

NOTES: 'All Races' includes other races and ethnic groups not shown separately.

UNITS: Civilian noninstitutional population and civilian labor force in thousands of persons; participation rate as a percent (the civilian noninstitutional population divided by the civilian labor force).

Table 6.03 Employed Members of the Civilian Labor Force, by Sex and Age, 2005

	Asian		White		All Races	
	male	female	male	female	male	female
2005						
all employed persons 16 years old and over	3,359	2,885	63,763	53,186	75,973	65,757
- persons 16-19 years old	67	73	2,508	2,597	2,923	3,055
- persons 20-24 years old	254	250	6,041	5,190	7,279	6,513
- persons 25-54 years old	2,563	2,154	44,194	36,152	53,201	45,315
- persons 55-64 years old	385	335	8,471	7,317	9,714	8,635
- persons 65 years old and over	91	74	2,550	1,930	2,857	2,238

SOURCE: U.S. Department of Labor, Bureau of Labor Statistics, *Employment and Earnings*, 2006; pp. 205-208, table 3; p. 209, table 4 (data from the Current Population Survey). L2.41/2:(vol)/1:(year)

NOTES: 'All Races' includes other races and ethnic groups not shown separately. Data covers members of the civilian labor force.

UNITS: Employed members of the civilian labor force in thousands of persons, by age group as shown.

Table 6.04 Employed Asian Persons as Percent of All Employed Persons in the Civilian Labor Force, by Selected Occupation, 2005

	Asian	All Races
2005		
All occupations	4.4%	141,730
Management occupations	4.2	14,685
chief executive	3.9	1,644
general and operations managers	3.6	872
computer and information systems managers	6.3	351
financial managers	6.3	1,045
education administrators	2.4	805
medical and health services managers	2.7	470
Business and financial operations occupations	9.8	5,765
accountants and auditors	9.8	1,683
insurance underwriters	2.6	110
wholesale and retail buyers, except farm products	1.9	213
Computer and mathematical occupations	14.7	3,246
computer scientists and systems analysts	11.4	745
database administrators	6.3	89
operations research analysts	6.2	86
Architecture and engineering occupations	9.9	2,793
architects, except naval	11.0	235
aerospace engineers	6.7	90
chemical engineers	15.2	55
civil engineers	10.3	319
engineering technicians, except drafters	7.0	410
Life, physical, and social science occupations	10.1	1,406
medical scientists	29.6	125
environmental scientists and geoscientists	1.9	99
psychologists	0.3	188
Legal occupations	2.6	1,614
lawyers	2.0	961
judges, magistrate, and other judicial workers	4.6	70
Education, training and library occupations	3.7	8,114
Healthcare practitioner and technical occupations	7.4	6,748
dentists	14.1	164
physicians and surgeons	17.3	830
registered nurses	6.4	2,416

continued on the next page

Table 6.04 continued

	Asian	All Races
Arts, design, entertainment, sports and media occupations	4.3%	2,736
Healthcare support occupations	4.1	3,092
Protective service occupations	1.6	2,894
fire fighters	1.4	243
police and sheriff's patrol officers	1.1	677
Food preparation and serving related occupations	5.4	7,374
Building and grounds cleaning and maintenance	2.7	5,241
Personal care and service occupations	6.0	4,531
Sales and related occupations	4.4	16,433
cashiers	5.4	3,075
retail salespersons	4.2	3,248
real estate brokers and sales agents	4.7	995
Office and administrative occupations	3.8	19,529
Farming, fishing and forestry occupations	1.6	976
Construction and extraction occupations	1.2	9,145
carpenters	1.1	1,797
construction laborers	1.2	1,491
electricians	1.7	852
Installation, maintenance and repair	3.0	5,226
Production occupations	4.9	9,378
electrical and electronic assemblers	16.1	209
machinist	3.6	420
printing machine operators	3.3	218
medical, dental, ophthalmic laboratory technicians	13.8	103
Transportation and material moving		8,664
aircraft pilots and flight engineers		121
bus drivers		591
industrial truck and tractor operators		541
refuse and recyclable material collectors		73

SOURCE: U.S. Department of Labor, Bureau of Labor Statistics, *Employment and Earnings*, January, 2006, pp. 218-223, table 11 (data from the Current Population Survey). L 2.41/2:408/1: (year)

NOTES: Only selected subcategories of occupational groups displayed.

UNITS: Employed Hispanic persons as a percent of all employed persons, by occupation. Employed persons in thousands.

Table 6.05 Employed Asian Persons as Percent of All Employed Persons in the Civilian Labor Force, by Industry Group, 2005

	Asian	All Races
2005		
All industries	4.4%	141,730
agriculture, forestry, fishing, and hunting	1.0	2,197
mining	1.3	624
construction	1.4	11,197
manufacturing	5.1	16,253
durable goods	5.7	10,333
nondurable goods	4.1	5,919
wholesale and retail trade	4.3	21,405
wholesale trade	4.3	4,579
retail trade	4.3	16,825
transportation and warehousing	4.0	6,184
utilities	1.5	1,176
information	4.8	3,402
finance and insurance	5.5	7,035
real estate and rental and leasing	3.3	3,168
legal services	2.7	1,658
architectural, engineering and related services	7.4	1,468
scientific research and development services	11.7	493
management, administrative and waste services	2.9	5,709
educational services	3.6	12,264
hospitals	6.8	5,719
health services, except hospitals	4.7	8,332
social assistance	3.1	2,860
arts, entertainment, and recreation	3.5	2,765
accommodation and food services	6.5	9,306
services	5.2	7,020

SOURCE: U.S. Department of Labor, Bureau of Labor Statistics, *Employment and Earnings*, January, 2006, pp. 234-238, table 18 (data from the Current Population Survey). L 2.41/2:40/1: (year)

NOTES: Only selected subcategories of industry groups are displayed.

UNITS: Employed Black persons as a percent of all employed persons, by industry group. Employ persons are 16 years and older and in thousands.

Table 6.06 Union Membership, by Sex, 2005

	Asian	White	All Races
Men			
total employed	2,881	54,462	65,466
members of unions			
number	314	7,275	8,870
as a percent of total employed	10.9%	13.4%	13.5%
represented by unions			
total	337	7,858	9,597
as a percent of total employed	11.7%	14.4%	14.7%
Women			
total employed	2,598	48,505	60,423
members of unions			
number	299	5,245	6,815
as a percent of total employed	11.5%	10.8%	11.3%
represented by unions			
total	329	5,897	7,626
as a percent of total employed	12.7%	12.2%	12.6%

SOURCE: U.S. Department of Labor, Bureau of Labor Statistics, *Employment and Earnings*, January 2006, p. 263, table 40, (data from the Current Population Survey). L 2.41/2:40/1: (year)

NOTES: 'All Races' includes other races/ethnic groups not shown separately. 'Members of unions' includes members of a labor union or an employee association similar to a union. 'Represented by unions' includes members of a labor union or an employee association similar to a union as well as workers who report no union affiliation but whose jobs are covered by a union or an employee association contract.

UNITS: Total employed, members of unions and represented by unions in thousands of persons 16 years old and older; percent as shown.

Table 6.07 Full-Time and Part-Time Status of Employed Persons in Nonagricultural Industries, 2005

	Asian	White	All Races
2005			
All employed persons in nonagricultural industries	6,037	110,298	134,115
full-time	4,884	83,589	102,397
part-time	1,153	26,709	31,717
part time for economic reasons	157	3,322	4,271

SOURCE: U.S. Department of Labor, Bureau of Labor Statistics, *Employment and Earnings*, January, 2006, p. 241, table 22 (data from the Current Population Survey). L 2.41/2:(vol)/1:(year)

NOTES: 'All Races' includes other races not shown separately. Economic reasons for persons who are employed part-time are: slack work; material shortages; repairs to plant or equipment; start or termination of a job during the week; and inability to find full time work.

UNITS: Employed members of the civilian labor force in thousands of persons, by status, as shown.

Table 6.08 Self-Employed Workers, 2003 - 2005

	Asian	White	All Races
2003	390	8,160	9,344
2004	411	8,252	9,467
2005	421	8,247	9,509

SOURCE: U.S. Department of Labor, Bureau of Labor Statistics, *Employment and Earnings*, January, 2004; p. 215, table 12; January, 2005; p. 216, table 12; January, 2006; p. 224, table 12 (data from the Current Population Survey).

NOTES: 'All Races' includes other races and ethnic groups not shown separately.

UNITS: Self-employed workers in thousands of persons.

Table 6.09 Work at Home, 2001 and 2004

	Asian	White	All Races
2001			
worked at home	na	3,138	3,436
percent who worked			
less than 8 hours	na	24.4%	24.5%
8 hours or more	na	48.0	47.6
35 hours or more	na	15.0	15.7
mean hours:			
worked at home	na	17.7	18.0
2004			
worked at home	102	2,999	3,349
percent distribution			
less than 8 hours	12.6%	20.9%	21.1%
8 hours or more	54.7	50.8	49.5
35 hours or more	16.9	15.3	14.8
mean hours:			
worked at home	21.1	19.0	18.6

SOURCE: U.S. Department of Labor, Bureau of Labor Statistics, "Table 3: Hours of paid job-related work at home on primary job among wage and salary workers"; May 2001; pp. 1-2, table 3; May 2004; table 3.

NOTES: Data refer to employed persons in nonagricultural industries who reported that they usually work at home at least once per week as part of their primary job excluding self-employed. Detail for the above race groups will not sum to totals because data for the "other races" group are not presented.

UNITS: Numbers in thousands of persons. Percent as a percent of persons working at home.

Table 6.10 Employment Status of Families, 2004-2005

	Asian	White	All Races
2004			
Total families	3,107	62,250	75,872
With employed member(s)	2,775	51,350	62,424
some usually work full time	2,630	47,620	57,813
With no employed member	332	10,900	13,447
With unemployed member(s)	208	4,078	5,593
some member(s) employed	171	3,000	3,915
some usually work full time	154	2,677	3,494
2005			
Total families	3,218	62,567	76,443
With employed member(s)	2,889	51,645	62,933
some usually work full time	2,741	47,883	58,276
With no employed member	329	10,922	13,509
With unemployed member(s)	199	3,801	5,318
some member(s) employed	160	2,782	3,717
some usually work full time	145	2,477	3,310

SOURCE: U.S. Department of Labor, Bureau Labor Statistics, "Employment and unemployment in families by race and Hispanic or Latino ethnicity, 2004-2005 annual averages"; <http://stats.bls.gov/news.release/famee.t01htm>; (accessed: 15 June 2004).

NOTES: 'All Races' includes other races and ethnic groups not shown separately.

UNITS: Number of families in thousands of families.

Table 6.11 Unemployment Rates for the Civilian Labor Force, by Age, 2005

	Asian	White	All Races
2005			
unemployment rate			
all ages	4.0%	4.4%	5.1%
- persons 16-19 years old	12.4	14.2	16.6
- persons 20-24 years old	6.5	7.2	8.8
- persons 25-54 years old	3.3	3.6	4.1
- persons 55-64 years old	4.9	3.0	3.3
- persons 65 years old and over	3.1	3.1	3.5

SOURCE: U.S. Department of Labor, Bureau of Labor Statistics, *Employment and Earnings*, 2006; pp. 205-208, table 3; p. 209, table 4 (data from the Current Population Survey). L2.41/2:(vol.)/1:(year)

NOTES: 'All Races' includes other races and ethnic groups not shown separately. Data covers members of the civilian labor force.

UNITS: Unemployment rate, by age group as shown.

Table 6.12 Unemployment Rates for the Civilian Labor Force, by Sex and Age, 2005

	Asian		White		All Races	
	male	female	male	female	male	female
2005						
unemployment rate						
all ages	4.0%	3.9%	4.4%	4.4%	5.1%	5.1%
- persons 16-19 years old	16.8	7.9	16.1	12.3	18.6	14.5
- persons 20-24 years old	9.0	3.8	7.9	6.4	9.6	7.9
- persons 25-54 years old	3.1	3.6	3.5	3.8	3.9	4.4
- persons 55-64 years old	4.3	5.6	3.0	3.0	3.3	3.3
- persons 65 years old and over	3.1	3.1	3.1	3.2	3.4	3.5

SOURCE: U.S. Department of Labor, Bureau of Labor Statistics, *Employment and Earnings*, 2006; pp. 205-208, table 3; p. 209, table 4 (data from the Current Population Survey). L2.41/2:(vol.)/1:(year)

NOTES: 'All Races' includes other races and ethnic groups not shown separately. Data covers members of the civilian labor force.

UNITS: Unemployment rate, by age group as shown.

Table 6.13 Unemployment, by Reason for Unemployment, 2005

	Asian	White	All Races
2005			
Total	259	5,350	7,591
job losers	104	2,681	3,667
job leavers	35	654	872
re-entrants to the labor force	92	1,589	2,386
new entrants to the labor force	28	425	666

SOURCE: U.S. Department of Labor, Bureau of Labor Statistics, *Employment and Earnings*, January, 2006; p. 247, table 27; p.248, table 29. (data from the Current Population Survey). L2.41/2:(vol)/1:(year)

NOTES: 'All Races' includes other races and ethnic groups not shown separately. Data covers members of the civilian labor force.

UNITS: Unemployed members of the civilian labor force in thousands of persons, by reason for unemployment as shown.

Table 6.14 Unemployed Jobseekers by Active Job Search Methods Used, 2005

	Asian	White	All Races
2005			
Total unemployed	259	5,350	7,591
Total jobseekers	245	4,595	6,657
Methods used as a percent of total jobseekers			
Employer directly	59.1%	61.1%	60.6%
Sent out resumes or filled out applications	47.1	55.6	55.4
Placed or answered ads	13.2	15.2	14.8
Friends or relatives	23.6	17.7	17.7
Public employment agency	16.7	17.2	18.3
Private employment agency	9.5	6.6	6.7
Other	16.2	11.6	11.1

SOURCE: U.S. Department of Labor, Bureau of Labor Statistics, *Employment and Earnings*, January, 2006, p. 252, table 33 (data from the Current Population Survey). L 2.41/2:40/1(year)

NOTES: 'All Races' includes other races not shown separately. "Jobseekers" does not include persons on temporary layoff.

UNITS: Persons in thousands of persons.

Chapter 7: Earnings, Income, Poverty & Wealth

Table 7.01 Per Capita Money Income, 2002 and 2003

	Asian	White	All Races
Median income			
2002	$24,131	$24,142	$22,794
2003	24,604	24,626	23,276

SOURCE: U.S. Bureau of the Census, Statistical Abstract of the United States: 2006; p. 467, table 687.

NOTES: 'All Races' includes other races and ethnic groups not shown separately. 'White' or 'Asian' is equivalent to 'White Alone' or 'Asian Alone' respectively; refers to people who reported 'White' or 'Asian' and did not report any other race category.

UNITS: In current dollars.

Table 7.02 Income of Persons from Specified Sources, 2004

	Asian	White	All Races
All persons, 15 years and over	8,208	169,478	205,146
Number with income from:			
Earnings	6,472	126,255	153,355
Unemployment compensation	215	5,046	6,354
Workers' compensation	71	1,666	2,087
Social Security	918	35,585	41,089
SSI (Supplemental Security Income)	199	3,645	5,334
Public assistance (total)	39	1,218	2,080
Veterans' benefits	32	2,211	2,575
Survivors benefits	37	2,483	2,743
Disability benefits	45	1,349	1,738
Pensions	317	14,213	15,901
Interest	3,849	86,292	97,651
Dividends	1,434	32,893	36,262
Rents, royalties, estates or trusts	418	10,262	11,409
Educational assistance	375	6,188	8,011
Child support	77	4,432	5,621
Alimony	19	449	505
Mean income, total from:	$39,320	$34,809	$33,846
Earnings	44,040	38,117	37,151
Unemployment compensation	4,168	3,865	3,932
Workers' compensation	na	6,290	6,113
Social Security	9,793	10,524	10,366
SSI (Supplemental Security Income)	6,857	5,668	5,730
Public assistance (total)	na	2,985	3,020
Veterans' benefits	na	10,216	10,236
Survivors benefits	na	11,744	12,087
Disability benefits	na	13,147	12,996
Pensions	16,593	15,650	15,615
Interest	1,796	1,715	1,675
Dividends	2,621	2,452	2,462
Rents, royalties, estates or trusts	6,814	6,143	6,074
Educational assistance	6,615	5,393	5,380
Child support	5,262	5,042	4,806
Alimony	na	12,435	11,936

SOURCE: U.S. Bureau of the Census and Bureau of Labor Statistics, Current Population Survey, Annual Demographic Survey, March Supplement, 2004; "(Table) PINC-09. Source of Income in 2004--Number With Income and Mean Income of Specified Type in 2004 of People 15 Years Old and Over, by Race, Hispanic Origin and Sex".

NOTES: 'All Races' includes other races and ethnic groups not shown separately. Persons 15 years old and older as of March the following year. 'White' and 'Asian' as shown here are equivalent to 'White Alone' and 'Asian Alone'.

UNITS: Number of persons in thousands

Table 7.03 Money Income of Persons 15 Years Old and Older, by Selected Characteristics, 2004

	Asian		White		All Races	
	male	female	male	female	male	female
Total with income	4,152	4,057	85,112	84,366	101,777	103,369
persons with incomes:						
$1-$2,499 or loss	196	495	4,019	8,311	4,969	9,997
$2,500-$4,999	105	234	2,168	4,662	2,831	5,894
$5,000-$7,499	175	300	3,050	6,885	4,084	8,565
$7,500-$9,999	161	232	3,145	5,949	3,969	7,429
$10,000-$12,499	186	257	4,111	6,623	5,156	7,966
$12,500-$14,999	126	169	3,431	4,651	3,969	5,627
$15,000-$17,499	202	195	4,251	4,892	5,201	5,985
$17,500-$19,999	138	102	3,102	3,549	3,770	4,290
$20,000-$22,499	169	208	4,362	4,554	5,298	5,676
$22,500-$24,999	109	121	2,803	2,928	3,334	3,584
$25,000-$27,499	204	169	3,677	3,734	4,572	4,686
$27,500-$29,999	88	75	2,225	2,116	2,694	2,642
$30,000-$32,499	204	180	4,142	3,497	5,089	4,460
$32,500-$34,999	89	56	1,869	1,762	2,167	2,123
$35,000-$37,499	148	147	3,433	2,602	4,093	3,188
$37,500-$39,999	62	64	1,727	1,467	2,042	1,812
$40,000-$42,499	170	144	3,534	2,384	4,200	2,950
$42,500-$44,999	44	28	1,488	1,047	1,681	1,202
$45,000-$47,499	104	80	2,337	1,455	2,725	1,714
$47,500-$49,999	52	67	1,470	967	1,677	1,182
$50,000-$52,499	174	103	2,826	1,494	3,371	1,811
$52,500-$54,999	45	34	978	619	1,135	740
$55,000-$57,499	62	70	1,663	825	1,915	1,015
$57,500-$59,999	52	11	821	495	955	562

continued on the next page

Table 7.03 continued

	Asian		White		All Races	
	male	female	male	female	male	female
$60,000-$62,499	99	72	1,933	905	2,205	1,127
$62,500-$64,999	41	28	771	429	874	538
$65,000-$67,499	50	44	1,274	604	1,449	726
$67,500-$69,999	9	15	635	377	680	427
$70,000-$72,499	74	42	1,252	555	1,425	672
$72,500-$74,999	26	19	543	238	611	292
$75,000-$77,499	74	34	1,024	426	1,186	507
$77,500-$79,999	13	9	498	222	545	266
$80,000-$82,499	85	37	955	370	1,099	444
$82,500-$84,999	22	5	360	208	409	240
$85,000-$87,499	30	24	618	223	683	259
$87,500-$89,999	13	5	354	132	383	156
$90,000-$92,499	37	16	623	243	723	280
$92,500-$94,999	12	10	284	103	315	131
$95,000-$97,499	52	5	439	138	546	157
$97,500-$99,999	14	6	268	93	297	107
$100,000 and over	438	145	6,650	1,630	7,452	1,939
median income	$32,886	$20,533	$31,335	$17,648	$30,513	$17,629
mean income	$48,791	$29,627	$44,305	$25,229	$42,832	$24,998

SOURCE: U.S. Bureau of the Census and Bureau of Labor Statistics, Current Population Survey, 2005 Annual social and Economic Supplement, Annual Demographic Survey, March Supplement; "(Table) PINC-01 Selected Characteristics of People 15 Years and Over, by Total Money Income in 2004, Work Experience in 2004, Race, Hispanic Origin, and Sex".

NOTES: 'All Races' includes other races and ethnic groups not shown separately. Number of persons as of March of the following year. 'White' and 'Asian' as shown are equivalent to 'White Alone' and 'Asian Alone' respectively that refer to people who reported 'White' or 'Asian' and did not report any other race category.

UNITS: Number of persons with income, in thousands of persons; mean and median income in current dollars.

Table 7.04 Median Income of Year-Round, Full-Time Workers, by Sex, 2003 - 2004

	Asian		White		All Races	
	male	female	male	female	male	female
2003	$46,220	$34,584	$42,142	$32,192	$41,503	$31,653
2004	46,690	36,595	42,601	32,683	41,667	32,101

SOURCE: U.S. Bureau of the Census and Bureau of Labor Statistics, Annual Demographic Survey, March Supplement, 2002, "(Table) PINC-01 Selected Characteristics of People 15 Years and Over, by Total Money Income in 2002, Work Experience in 2002, Race, Hispanic Origin, and Sex";2003; 2004.

NOTES: 'All Races' includes other races/ethnic groups not shown separately. Data covers the earnings of wage and salary workers who usually worked 35 or more hours per week for 50 to 52 weeks during the year. 'White' and 'Asian' as shown are equivalent to 'White Alone' and 'Asian Alone' respectively; that refer to people who reported 'White' or 'Asian' and did not report any other race category.

UNITS: Median money earnings.

Table 7.05 Median Weekly Earnings of Full-Time and Part-Time Wage and Salary Workers, by Sex and Age, 2005

	Asian		White		All Races	
	male	female	male	female	male	female
Full-Time Wage and Salary Workers						
All full-time wage and salary workers	$825	$665	$743	$596	$722	$585
workers 16-24 years old	na	na	na	na	409	381
workers 25 years old and over	na	na	na	na	771	612
Part-Time Wage and Salary Workers						
All part-time wage and salary workers	$190	$210	$190	$208	$190	$206
workers 16-24 years old	na	na	na	na	151	147
workers 25 years old and over	na	na	na	na	250	245

SOURCE: U.S. Department of Labor, Bureau of Labor Statistics, *Employment and Earnings*, January, 2006; p. 256, table 37; p. 257, table 38 (data from the Current Population Survey). L 2.41/2:38/1:(year)

NOTES: 'All Races' includes other races not shown separately.

UNITS: Median weekly earning in dollars.

Table 7.06 Money Income of Households, 2002 and 2003

	Asian	White	All Races
Median income			
2002	$52,626	$45,086	$42,409
2003	55,699	45,631	43,318

SOURCE: U.S. Bureau of the Census, Statistical Abstract of the United States: 2006; p. 460, table 674.

NOTES: 'All Races' includes other races and ethnic groups not shown separately. 'White' or 'Asian' is equivalent to 'White Alone' or 'Asian Alone' respectively; refers to people who reported 'White' or 'Asian' and did not report any other race category.

UNITS: In current dollars.

Table 7.07 Money Income of Households, by Income Interval, 2003

	Asian	White	All Races
Number of households	4,040	91,692	112,000
with current dollar incomes of:			
under $10,000	432	7,012	10,111
$10,000 - $14,999	181	6,035	7,740
$15,000 - $19,999	231	5,926	7,434
$20,000 - $24,999	153	5,827	7,215
$25,000 - $29,999	124	5,479	6,718
$30,000 - $34,999	162	5,412	6,559
$35,000 - $39,999	187	4,954	6,024
$40,000 - $44,999	199	4,765	5,801
$45,000 - $49,999	172	4,096	4,948
$50,000 - $59,999	299	7,676	9,151
$60,000 - $74,999	445	9,346	11,040
$75,000 - $84,999	246	4,993	5,815
$85,000 - $99,999	260	5,619	6,498
$100,000 - $149,999	575	9,309	10,719
$150,000 - $199,999	234	2,933	3,372
$200,000 - $249,999	67	1,157	1,307
$250,000 and above	71	1,421	1,547

SOURCE: U.S. Census Bureau, Statistical Abstract of the United States: 2006; p 462, table 676.

NOTES: 'All Races' includes other races not shown separately. Number of families as of March of the following year. 'Asian' and 'White' refer to persons who selected this race group only and excludes persons reporting more than one race.

UNITS: Number of households in thousands.

Table 7.08 Money Income of Families, 2003 - 2004

	Asian	White	All Races
Median income			
2003	$63,251	$55,768	$52,680
2004	65,482	56,700	54,061
Mean income			
2003	$77,513	$71,770	$68,563
2004	85,505	73,395	70,402

SOURCE: U.S. Bureau of the Census, Current Population Reports: Historical Income Tables - Families, "(Table) F-23. Families by Total Money Income, Race, and Hispanic Origin of Householder: 1967 to 2003;" published September 2003.
U.S. Bureau of the Census, Current Population Reports: Income 2003; "(Table) FINC-01. Selected Characteristics of Families by Total Money Income in 2003"; 2004.

NOTES: 'All Races' includes other races and ethnic groups not shown separately. 'White' or 'Asian' is equivalent to 'White Alone' or 'Asian Alone' respectively; refers to people who reported 'White' or 'Asian' and did not report any other race category.

UNITS: In current dollars.

Table 7.09 Money Income of Families, by Selected Family Characteristics, 2004

	Asian	White	All Races
Families			
Number of families	3,155	63,227	77,019
with current dollar incomes of:			
under $5,000	58	1,408	2,185
$5,000-$9,999	63	1,328	2,072
$10,000-$14,999	77	2,270	3,060
$15,000-$24,999	244	6,407	8,241
$25,000-$34,999	270	6,682	8,378
$35,000-$49,999	447	9,292	11,407
$50,000-$74,999	635	13,353	15,836
$75,000-$99,999	429	8,919	10,338
$100,000 and over	933	13,569	15,502
median income	$65,482	$56,700	$54,061
mean income	$85,505	$73,395	$70,402
Median income by:			
type of family			
married couple families	$72,249	$64,443	$63,630
wife in paid labor force	85,251	78,117	76,814
wife not in paid labor force	54,883	42,530	42,221
male householder, no wife present	46,927	41,333	40,293
female householder, no husband present	39,741	29,112	26,964

continued on the next page

Table 7.09 continued

	Asian	White	All Races
Median income by:			
age of householder			
15-24 years old	$36,180	$29,379	$26,451
25-34 years old	65,184	49,636	46,878
35-44 years old	76,948	65,630	62,121
45-54 years old	67,652	75,042	71,002
55-64 years old	66,605	64,631	62,176
65 years old and over	40,120	36,637	35,825
size of family			
two persons	$52,281	$47,680	$45,819
three persons	65,020	60,788	56,709
four persons	80,990	69,694	66,111
five persons	73,579	64,837	52,552
six persons	77,107	60,263	56,296
seven or more persons	68,687	61,738	57,653
number of earners			
no earners	$18,698	$24,627	$22,349
one earner	50,581	40,313	37,618
two earners or more	82,340	76,564	75,023

SOURCE: U.S. Bureau of the Census, Current Population Reports: Income 2004; "(Table) FINC-01. Selected Characteristics of Families by Total Money Income in 2004".

NOTES: 'All Races' includes other races not shown separately. Number of families as of March of the following year. 'White' as shown is equivalent to 'White Alone' that refers to people who reported 'White' and did not report any other race category.

UNITS: Number of families and families with income, in thousands of families; mean and median income in current dollars.

Table 7.10 Persons Below the Poverty Level, 1987 – 2004

	Asian	White	All Races
Number below the poverty level			
1987	1,021	22,860	33,064
1990	858	22,326	33,585
1995	1,411	24,423	36,425
2000	1,258	21,291	31,139
2001	1,275	22,739	32,907
2002*	1,161	23,466	34,570
2003*	1,401	24,272	35,861
2004*	1,209	25,301	36,997
Percent below the poverty level			
1987	16.1%	11.4%	14.0%
1990	12.2	10.7	13.5
1995	14.6	11.2	13.8
2000	9.9	9.4	11.3
2001	10.2	9.9	11.7
2002*	10.1	10.2	12.1
2003*	11.8	10.5	12.5
2004*	9.8	10.8	12.7

SOURCE: U.S. Bureau of the Census, Current Population Reports: Income, Poverty, and Health Insurance Coverage in the United States: 2004; Series P-60, #229; Table B-1; issued August 2005.

NOTES: 'All Races' includes other races and ethnic groups not shown separately. '*' indicates the year in which 'White' or 'Asian' as shown is equivalent to 'White Alone' or 'Asian Alone' that refers to people who reported 'White' or 'Asian' and did not report any other race category. Otherwise, 'Asian' is equivalent to 'Asian or Pacific Islander'.

UNITS: Number below the poverty level in thousands of persons; percent as a percent of all persons, by race, as shown.

Table 7.11 Children Below the Poverty Level, 1987 - 2004

	Asian	White	All Races
Number below the poverty level			
1987	455	7,788	12,843
1990	374	8,232	13,431
1995	564	8,981	14,665
2000	420	7,328	11,633
2001	369	7,527	11,733
2002*	315	7,549	12,133
2003*	344	7,985	12,866
2004*	286	8,299	13,027
Percent below the poverty level			
1987	23.5%	15.3%	20.3%
1990	17.6	15.9	20.6
1995	19.5	16.2	20.8
2000	12.7	13.0	16.2
2001	11.5	13.4	16.3
2002*	11.7	13.6	16.7
2003*	12.5	14.3	17.6
2004*	10.0	14.8	17.8

SOURCE: U.S. Bureau of the Census, Current Population Reports: Income, Poverty, and Health Insurance Coverage in the United States: 2004; Series P-60, #229; Table B-2; issued August 2005.

NOTES: 'All Races' includes other races and ethnic groups not shown separately. '*' indicates the year in which 'White' or 'Asian' as shown is equivalent to 'White Alone' or 'Asian Alone' that refers to people who reported 'White' or 'Asian' and did not report any other race category. Otherwise, 'Asian' is equivalent to 'Asian or Pacific Islander'.

UNITS: Number below the poverty level in thousands of children; percent as a percent of all children under 18 years, by race, as shown.

Table 7.12 Persons 65 Years Old and Over Below the Poverty Level, 1987 - 2004

	Asian	White	All Races
Number below the poverty level			
1987	56	2,704	3,563
1990	62	2,707	3,658
1995	89	2,572	3,318
2000	82	2,601	3,359
2001	92	2,656	3,414
2002*	82	2,739	3,576
2003*	151	2,666	3,552
2004*	148	2,537	3,457
Percent below the poverty level			
1987	15.0%	10.6%	12.5%
1990	12.1	10.1	12.2
1995	14.3	9.0	10.5
2000	9.3	8.7	10.2
2001	10.2	8.9	10.1
2002*	8.4	9.1	10.4
2003*	14.3	8.8	10.2
2004*	13.6	8.3	9.8

SOURCE: U.S. Bureau of the Census, Current Population Reports: Income, Poverty, and Health Insurance Coverage in the United States: 2003; Series P-60, #229; Table B-2; issued August 2005.

NOTES: 'All Races' includes other races not shown separately. '*' indicates the year in which 'White' as shown is respectively equivalent to 'White Alone' that refers to people who reported 'White' and did not report any other race category.

UNITS: Number below the poverty level in thousands of persons; percent as a percent of all persons, by race, as shown.

Table 7.13 Families Below the Poverty Level by Type of Family and Presence of Related Children, 2003 and 2004

	Asian	White	All Races
2003			
Total Families	3,064	62,620	76,232
Families below poverty level	311	5,058	7,607
Married-couple families	200	2,504	3,115
Male householder, no wife present	28	383	636
Female householder, no husband present	83	2,171	3,856
Total families with children under 18 years	1,755	30,443	39,029
Families below poverty level	193	3,698	5,772
Married-couple families	119	1,499	1,885
Male householder, no wife present	12	287	470
Female householder, no husband present	62	1,912	3,416
2004			
Total Families	3,155	63,227	77,019
Families below poverty level	232	5,315	7,854
Married-couple families	147	2,591	3,222
Male householder, no wife present	38	435	658
Female householder, no husband present	48	2,288	3,973
Total families with children under 18 years	1,774	31,212	39,710
Families below poverty level	147	3,866	5,847
Married-couple families	95	1,540	1,915
Male householder, no wife present	15	305	443
Female householder, no husband present	37	2,021	3,489

SOURCE: U.S. Bureau of the Census, Current Population Reports: Poverty in the United States: 2003; "Table POV44: Region, Division and Type of Residence – Poverty Status for Families by Family Structure: 2003, Below 100% of Poverty"; Table POV45: Region, Division and Type of Residence – Poverty Status for Families With Related Children Under 18 by Family Structure: 2003, Below 100% of Poverty"; 2004.

NOTES: 'All Races' includes other races not shown separately. 'White' as shown is equivalent to 'White Alone' that refer to people who reported 'White' and did not report any other race category.

UNITS: Number in thousands of families

Chapter 8: Crime & Corrections

Table 8.01 Victimization Rates for Personal Crimes, by Type of Crime, 2002

	Asian	White	All Races
All personal crimes	16.9	22.1	23.3
Crimes of violence	16.0	21.5	22.6
completed	6.2	6.1	6.9
attempted/threatened	9.8	15.4	15.7
rape/sexual assault	0.2*	0.8	0.8
rape/attempted rape	0.0*	0.4	0.5
- rape	0.0*	0.3	0.3
- attempted rape	0.0*	0.2	0.2
sexual assault	0.2*	0.4	0.3
robbery	3.4	1.9	2.5
completed/property taken	2.3*	1.1	1.6
- with injury	1.8*	0.5	0.7
- without injury	0.5*	0.6	0.9
attempted to take property	1.1*	0.8	0.9
- with injury	0.0*	0.2	0.2
- without injury	1.1*	0.6	0.7
assault	12.4	18.8	19.3
aggravated	5.4	4.2	4.6
- with injury	2.5*	1.3	1.5
- threatened with weapon	2.9*	2.8	3.1
simple	7.0	14.7	14.6
- with minor injury	1.4*	3.1	3.2
- without injury	5.7	11.6	11.4
purse snatching/pocket picking	0.9*	0.6	0.8

SOURCE: U.S. Department of Justice, Bureau of Justice Statistics, Sourcebook of Criminal Justice Statistics 2003; table 3.8, table 3.9.

NOTES: 'All Races' includes other races not shown separately. 'Asian' includes American Indian, Eskimo, Asian and Pacific Islander if only one of these races is given. 'Attempted rape' and 'sexual assault' include threats. The National Crime Victimization Survey has been redesigned. Comparisons of estimates of crime based on previous survey procedures (before 1993) are not recommended. * Based on 10 or fewer sample cases.

UNITS: Rates per 1,000 persons, 12 years old and over.

Table 8.02 Victimization Rates for Property Crimes, by Type of Crime, 2003

	Asian households	White households	All Races households
All property crimes	141.7	159.1	163.2
Household burglary	28.5	28.4	29.8
completed	23.4	23.7	24.6
- forcible entry	11.3	7.8	8.9
- unlawful entry without force	12.1	15.9	15.7
attempted forcible entry	5.1*	4.6	5.1
Theft	99.8	122.9	124.4
completed	96.4	118.6	120.2
- less than $50.	24.2	37.1	36.7
- $50-$249	35.9	40.6	41.6
- $250 or more	24.8	29.7	29.6
- amount not available	11.4	11.2	12.3
attempted	3.5*	4.3	4.2
Motor vehicle theft	13.3	7.8	9.0
completed	10.6	6.0	6.7
attempted	2.7*	1.8	2.4

SOURCE: U.S. Department of Justice, Bureau of Justice Statistics, Sourcebook of Criminal Justice Statistics 2003, table 3.22.2003.

NOTES: 'All races households' includes households of other races not shown separately. 'Asian' includes American Indian, Eskimo, Asian and Pacific Islander if only one of these races is given. * - estimate is based on about 10 or fewer samples cases. The National Crime Victimization Survey has been redesigned. Comparisons of estimates of crime based on previous survey procedures (before 1993) are not recommended.

UNITS: Rates per 1,000 households.

Table 8.03 Hate Crimes, Race as Bias Motivation, 2000 - 2003

	Anti-Asian	Race-Motivation Total	Total Hate Crimes
2000 – 2003	232	3,859	33,084

SOURCE: U.S. Census Bureau, Statistical Abstract of the United States, 2006; table 305 (data from *Hate Crime Statistics, 2004*, FBI Uniform Crime Reports.)

NOTES: 'Asian' includes Asian or Pacific Islander.

UNITS: Number of incidents reported.

Table 8.04 Race of Suspected Offender in Hate Crimes, 2004

	Asian	White	All Races
2004			
Bias motivation			
total	61	3,720	9,035
race	33	2,234	4,863
ethnicity	12	574	1,201
religion	7	292	1,480
sexual orientation	9	590	1,406
disability	0	22	71
multiple biases*	0	8	14

SOURCE: U.S. Department of Justice, Bureau of Justice Statistics, Sourcebook of Criminal Justice Statistics, 2004; table 3.114 (data from *Hate Crime Statistics, 2004*, FBI Uniform Crime Reports.)

NOTES: 'All Races' includes other races not shown separately. 'Asian' includes Asian or Pacific Islander. *A hate crime in which two or more offense types were committed as a result of two or more bias motivations.

UNITS: Number of incidents.

Table 8.05 Death Rates for Firearm-Related Injuries, 2000 and 2003

	Asian		White		All Races
	male	female	male	female	both sexes
2000					
All ages	6.0	1.1	15.9	2.7	10.2
15-24 years	9.3	*	19.6	2.8	16.8
25-44 years	8.1	1.5	18.0	3.9	13.1
45-64 years	7.4	*	17.4	3.5	10.0
65 years and over	*	*	28.2	2.4	12.2
2003					
All ages	5.4	1.1	16.0	2.6	10.3
15-24 years	10.5	2.1	19.2	2.5	16.6
25-44 years	6.9	1.3	18.1	3.6	13.4
45-64 years	5.7	1.5	19.0	3.7	10.7
65 years and over	*	*	27.4	2.1	11.8

SOURCE: U.S. Department of Health and Human Services, Health, United States, 2005 (Centers for Disease Control and Prevention, National Center for Health Statistics), pp. 224-226, table 47.

NOTES: 'All Races' includes other races not shown separately. 'Asian' includes Asian or Pacific Islander. Death rates for the Asian or Pacific Islander populations are known to be underestimated. *Indicates data based on fewer than 20 deaths.

UNITS: Death rate per 100,000 population.

Table 8.06 Law Enforcement Officers Killed, 1984 - 2004

	Asian	White	All Races	
1984	1	85	100%	(72)
1985	1	88	"	(78)
1986	0	89	"	(66)
1987	0	90	"	(73)
1988	0	91	"	(78)
1989	0	89	"	(66)
1990	2	80	"	(65)
1991	0	87	"	(71)
1992	2	82	"	(62)
1993	0	86	"	(70)
1994	1	84	"	(76)
1995	4	84	"	(74)
1996	5	80	"	(55)
1997	3	80	"	(65)
1998	2	87	"	(61)
1999	5	88	"	(42)
2000	0	76	"	(51)
2001	1	87	"	(70*)
2002	2	91	"	(56)
2003	6	79	"	(52)
2004	2	81	"	(57)

SOURCE: U.S. Department of Justice, Bureau of Justice Statistics, Sourcebook of Criminal Justice Statistics, 2004, table 3.158 (data from Federal Bureau of Investigation, *Law Enforcement Officers Killed and Assaulted, {annual}*).

NOTES: 'All Races' includes other races not shown separately. 'Asian' includes Asian, Pacific Islander, American Indian and Alaskan Native. Data have been revised since last publication. (xx) where xx denotes the total. '*' does not include the deaths of 72 law enforcement officers (12 Black and 59 White) resulting from the events of Sept. 11, 2001.

UNITS: Percent distribution of law enforcement officers killed as a percent of total, 100.0% (total number of law enforcement officers killed shown in parenthesis).

Table 8.07 Arrests, by Offense Charged, 2004

	number of arrests			percent distribution		
	Asian	White	All Races	Asian	White	All Races
All arrests	106,846	7,042,510	9,940,671	1.1%	70.8%	100.0%
Arrests for violent crimes	4,590	255,466	419,336	1.1	60.9	"
Arrests for property crimes	15,938	819,732	1,183,580	1.3	69.3	"
arrests for violent crimes:						
murder and nonnegligent manslaughter	117	4,816	9,539	1.2	50.5	"
forcible rape	208	12,140	18,489	1.1	65.7	"
robbery	716	35,439	78,397	0.6	45.2	"
aggravated assault	3,549	203,071	312,911	1.3	64.9	"
arrests for property crimes:						
burglary	2,023	149,525	210,577	1.0	71.0	"
larceny-theft	12,266	594,742	856,521	1.4	69.4	"
motor vehicle theft	1,510	66,948	105,466	1.4	63.5	"
arson	139	8,517	11,016	1.3	77.3	"

SOURCE: U.S. Federal Bureau of Investigation, Crime in the United States 2004, p. 298, table 43, updated 2/17/06 (data from the Uniform Crime Reporting program).

NOTES: 'All Races' includes other races not shown separately. 'Asian' includes Asian or Pacific Islander. Crime index crimes are made up of the four violent crimes (murder and nonnegligent manslaughter, rape, robbery, and aggravated assault), and four property crimes (burglary, larceny-theft, motor vehicle theft, and arson) which are tracked by the FBI.

UNITS: Number of arrests; percent distribution as a percent of total, 100.0%

Table 8.08 Arrests in Cities, by Offense Charged, 2004

	number of arrests			percent distribution		
	Asian	White	All Races	Asian	White	All Races
All arrests	86,740	5,107,931	7,456,479	1.2%	68.5%	100.0%
arrests for violent crimes	3,764	185,665	321,100	1.2	57.8	"
arrests for property crimes	13,466	654,823	962,087	1.4	68.1	"
arrests for violent crimes:						
murder and nonnegligent manslaughter	101	3,146	7,034	1.4	42.5	"
forcible rape	168	7,879	13,034	1.3	58.7	"
robbery	621	29,238	66,344	0.9	42.8	"
aggravated assault	2,874	145,402	234,688	1.2	61.7	"
arrests for property crimes:						
burglary	1,583	104,006	153,425	1.0	67.2	"
larceny-theft	10,543	495,885	718,965	1.5	67.9	"
motor vehicle theft	1,242	49,030	81,880	1.5	57.4	"
arson	98	5,902	7,817	1.3	74.7	"

SOURCE: U.S. Federal Bureau of Investigation, Crime in the United States 2004; p. 307, table 49, data updated 2/17/06 (data from the Uniform Crime Reporting program).

NOTES: 'All Races' includes other races not shown separately. 'Asian' includes Asian or Pacific Islander. Crime index crimes are made up of the four violent crimes (murder and nonnegligent manslaughter, rape, robbery, and aggravated assault), and four property crimes (burglary, larceny-theft, motor vehicle theft, and arson) which are tracked by the FBI.

UNITS: Number of arrests; percent distribution as a percent of total, 100.0%

Table 8.09 Jail Inmates, 1990, 1995 and 2000 - 2005

	Asian	White	All Races
1990	1.3%	41.8%	100%
1995	1.7	40.1	"
2000	1.6	41.9	"
2001	1.6	43.0	"
2002	1.6	43.8	"
2003	1.8	43.6	"
2004	1.8	44.4	"
2005	1.8	44.3	"

SOURCE: U.S. Department of Justice, Bureau of Justice Statistics, Prison and Jail Inmates 2001; p. 9, table 11; 2004; p. 8, table 10; Sourcebook of Criminal Justice Statistics 2005, table 6.17.

NOTES: 'All Races' includes other races and ethnic groups not shown separately. 'White' excludes Hispanic persons. 'Asian' includes Asians, American Indians, Alaska Natives, Native Hawaiians and other Pacific Islanders.

UNITS: Percent of local jail inmates.

Table 8.10 Prisoners Under Jurisdiction of Federal and State Correctional Authorities, 1995, 2000 – 2004

	Asian	White	All Races
June 30, 2000			
total	9,670	453,300	1,305,253
federal institutions	1,480	29,800	110,974
state institutions	6,527	395,637	1,101,202
private institutions	1,662	27,905	93,077
December 31, 2001			
total	na	na	1,404,032
federal institutions	na	na	156,993
state institutions	na	na	1,247,039
December 31, 2002			
total	na	na	1,440,144
federal institutions	na	na	163,528
state institutions	na	na	1,276,616
December 31, 2003			
total	na	na	1,468,601
federal institutions	na	na	173,059
state institutions	na	na	1,295,542
December 31, 2004			
total	na	na	1,496,629
federal institutions	na	na	180,328
state institutions	na	na	1,316,301

SOURCE: U.S. Department of Justice, Bureau of Justice Statistics, Sourcebook of Criminal Justice Statistics, 2002, table 6.24, table 6.28; 2004; table 6.30.

NOTES: 'All Races' includes other races and ethnic groups not shown separately. 'Asian' includes Asian, Pacific Islander or Native Hawaiian. 'White' excludes Hispanic persons.

UNITS: Number of prisoners under jurisdictional authority.

Table 8.11 Prisoners Under Sentence of Death, by State, January 1, 2006

	Asian	White	All Races
United States*	38	1,531	3,373
Alabama	0	94	190
Arizona	0	89	125
Arkansas	0	14	38
California	21	251	649
Colorado	0	0	2
Connecticut	0	3	8
Delaware	0	9	18
Florida	1	216	388
Georgia	1	54	109
Idaho	0	20	20
Illinois	0	5	10
Indiana	0	18	26
Kansas	0	5	8
Kentucky	0	28	37
Louisiana	1	28	85
Maryland	0	3	8
Mississippi	1	31	65
Missouri	0	31	53
Montana	0	4	4
Nebraska	0	6	10
Nevada	1	42	83
New Hampshire	--	--	0
New Jersey	0	7	13
New Mexico	0	2	2
New York	0	0	1
North Carolina	1	72	190
Ohio	2	91	196
Oklahoma	0	51	191
Oregon	0	26	33
Pennsylvania	2	71	231
South Carolina	0	36	74
South Dakota	0	4	4
Tennessee	2	60	108
Texas	4	124	409
Utah	0	6	9
Virginia	0	10	22
Washington	0	6	10
Wyoming	0	2	2

SOURCE: U.S. Department of Justice, Bureau of Justice Statistics, Sourcebook of Criminal Justice Statistics, 2004; table 6.77. Data from NAACP Legal Defense and Educational Fund. J 29.9/6: (year)

NOTES: 'All Races' includes other races and ethnic groups not shown separately. * Includes prisoners under Federal and U.S. Military jurisdiction.

UNITS: Number prisoners under sentence of death.

Table 8.12 Attitudes Toward the Death Penalty, 2004-2005

Question: "Are you in favor of the death penalty for a person convicted of murder?"

	Non-white	White	All Races
Yes, in favor	49%	69%	64%
No, not in favor	41	26	30
Don't know / refused	10	5	6

Question: "Generally speaking, do you believe the death penalty is applied fairly or unfairly in this country today?"

	Non-white	White	All Races
Applied fairly	41%	59%	55%
Applied unfairly	51	35	39
Don't know / refused	8	6	6

Question: "Do you feel that the death penalty acts as a deterrent to the commitment of murder, that it lowers the murder rate, or not?"

	Non-white	White	All Races
Yes, does	31%	37%	35%
No, does not	64	61	62
Don't know / refused	5	2	3

SOURCE: U.S. Department of Justice, Bureau of Justice Statistics, Sourcebook of Criminal Justice Statistics; tables 2.52.2005, 2.54, 2.58.

NOTES: Table constructed by Sourcebook staff from data provided by The Gallup Organization, Inc. 'Nonwhite' includes Black.

UNITS: Percent of persons taking survey who answered with given response.

Table 8.13 Students Who Reported Carrying a Weapon, 1999, 2001 and 2003

	Asian	White	All Races
1999			
anywhere	13.0%	16.4%	17.3%
on school property	6.5	6.4	6.9
2001			
anywhere	10.6%	17.9%	17.4%
on school property	7.2	6.1	6.4
2003			
anywhere	11.6%	16.7%	17.1%
on school property	6.6	5.5	6.1

SOURCE: U.S. Department of Justice, Bureau of Justice Statistics, Sourcebook of Criminal Justice Statistics, 2004, table 3.158 (data from Federal Bureau of Investigation, *Law Enforcement Officers Killed and Assaulted, {annual}*).

NOTES: 'All Races' includes other races not shown separately. 'White' includes non-hispanic White only. Weapons are such things as guns, knives and clubs.

UNITS: Percent, for students in grades 9 to 12.

Table 8.14 Type of Offense by Juvenile Offenders, 1999 and 2000

	Asian	White	All Races
1999			
All offenses	3.4%	68.2%	100%
Person	2.9	62.7	100
Property	4.1	70.1	100
Drug	2.3	71.1	100
Public order	3.0	69.0	100
2000			
All offenses	3.3%	68.6%	100%
Person	3.0	61.9	100
Property	4.0	69.7	100
Drug	2.4	75.4	100
Public order	3.1	69.6	100

SOURCE: U.S. Department of Justice, Bureau of Justice Statistics, Sourcebook of Criminal Justice Statistics, 2001; p. 455, table 5.59; 2002; table 5.61.

NOTES: 'Asian' includes original peoples of North America and Pacific Islanders. 'All Races' includes other races not shown separately. Cases disposed by juvenile courts.

UNITS: Percent of all offenses committed by juvenile offenders, as disposed by juvenile courts.

Table 8.15 Arrests, by Offense Charged, Persons Under 18 Years of Age, 2004

	number of arrests			percent distribution		
	Asian	White	All Races	Asian	White	All Races
All arrests	22,625	1,099,562	1,574,812	1.4%	69.8%	100.0%
arrests for violent crimes	809	34,049	65,163	1.2	52.3	"
arrests for property crimes	5,807	223,819	325,285	1.8	68.8	"
arrests for violent crimes:						
murder and nonnegligent manslaughter	11	372	782	1.4	47.6	"
forcible rape	25	1,908	2,992	0.8	63.8	"
robbery	261	6,398	18,226	1.4	35.1	"
aggravated assault	512	25,371	43,163	1.2	58.8	"
arrests for property crimes:						
burglary	674	41,032	58,318	1.2	70.4	"
larceny-theft	4,586	162,533	233,501	2.0	69.6	"
motor vehicle theft	472	15,903	27,937	1.7	56.9	"
arson	75	4,351	5,529	1.4	78.7	"

SOURCE: U.S. Federal Bureau of Investigation, Crime in the United States 2004; p. 299, table 43, data updated 2/17/06 (data from the Uniform Crime Reporting program).

NOTES: 'All Races' includes other races not shown separately. 'Asian' includes Asian or Pacific Islander. Crime index crimes are made up of the four violent crimes (murder and nonnegligent manslaughter, rape, robbery, and aggravated assault), and four property crimes (burglary, larceny-theft, motor vehicle theft, and arson) which are tracked by the FBI.

UNITS: Number of arrests; percent distribution as a percent of total, 100.0%

Table 8.16 Juvenile Court Cases, by Type of Case and Outcome, 2000

	Asian	White	All Races
Type of offense			
Total	100%	100%	100%
crimes against persons	20.3	20.6	22.8
crimes against property	48.7	41.6	40.9
drug law violations	8.6	13.2	12.0
offenses against public order	22.4	24.6	24.2
Case outcome			
Delinquency cases			
detained prior to court disposition	23.6	17.5%	19.5%
petitioned	55.3	55.1	57.8
Petitioned cases			
adjudicated delinquent	67.0	67.2	66.2
transferred/waived to adult court	na	0.5	0.6
Adjudicated cases			
placed out of home	22.5	22.8	24.0
placed on probation	64.3	63.6	63.1
dismissed	na	2.2	2.5
other	12.0	11.4	10.3

SOURCE: U.S. Department of Justice, Bureau of Justice Statistics, Sourcebook of Criminal Justice Statistics, 2002; table 5.62, table 5.63.
J 29.9/6:002

NOTES: 'Asian' includes original peoples of North America and Pacific Islanders. 'All Races' includes other races not shown separately. Data based on national estimates of delinquency cases disposed by juvenile courts.

UNITS: Percent, as a percent of total shown, 100.0%.

Chapter 9: Vital Statistics & Health

Table 9.01 Fertility Rates and Birth Rates, by Age of Mother, 1990, 2000, 2003 and 2004

	Asian women	White women	All women
1990			
Fertility rate	69.6	68.3	70.9
Birth rate per 1,000 women, by age group			
15-19 years old	26.4	50.8	59.9
20-24 years old	79.2	109.8	116.5
25-29 years old	126.3	120.7	120.2
30-34 years old	106.5	81.7	80.8
35-39 years old	49.6	31.5	31.7
40-44 years old	10.7	5.2	5.5
2000			
Fertility rate	65.8	65.3	65.9
Birth rate per 1,000 women, by age group			
15-19 years old	20.5	43.2	47.7
20-24 years old	60.3	106.6	109.7
25-29 years old	108.4	116.7	113.5
30-34 years old	116.5	94.6	91.2
35-39 years old	59.0	40.2	39.7
40-44 years old	12.6	7.9	8.0

continued on the next page

Table 9.01 continued

	Asian women	White women	All women
2003			
Births	221,203	3,225,848	4,089,950
Fertility rate	66.3	66.1	66.1
Birth rate per 1,000 women, by age group			
10-14 years old	0.2	0.5	0.6
15-19 years old	17.4	38.3	41.6
20-24 years old	59.6	100.6	102.6
25-29 years old	108.5	119.5	115.6
30-34 years old	114.6	99.3	95.1
35-39 years old	59.9	44.8	43.8
40-44 years old	13.5	8.7	8.7
45-54 years old	0.9	0.5	0.5
2004 (Preliminary)			
Births	229,352	3,229,814	4,115,590
Fertility rate	67.2	66.2	66.3
Birth rate per 1,000 women, by age group			
10-14 years old	0.2	0.5	0.7
15-19 years old	17.4	37.8	41.2
20-24 years old	60.1	99.4	101.8
25-29 years old	108.7	118.9	115.5
30-34 years old	116.9	99.3	95.5
35-39 years old	62.1	46.5	45.4
40-44 years old	13.7	8.9	9.0
45-54 years old	1.0	0.5	0.6

SOURCE: U.S. Department of Health and Human Services, Health United States, 2005; pp. 132-133, table 3 (Centers for Disease Control and Prevention, National Center for Health Statistics).

NOTES: 'Women of All Races' includes women of other races not shown separately. 'Asian' includes Asian or Pacific Islander. 'Fertility Rate' is total number of live births regardless of age of mother per 1,000 women, 15-44 years of age.

UNITS: Live births per 1,000 women

Table 9.02 Birth Rates by Live Birth Order, 2003 and 2004 (preliminary)

	Asian mothers	White mothers	All mothers
2003			
All live births	66.3	66.2	66.1
first child	31.3	26.7	26.7
second child	23.0	21.9	21.5
third child	7.9	11.1	11.0
fourth child and over	4.1	6.5	6.8
2004 (preliminary)			
All live births	67.2	66.2	66.3
first child	31.1	26.4	26.4
second child	23.4	21.7	21.4
third child	8.3	11.3	11.2
fourth child and over	4.3	6.9	7.3

SOURCE: U.S. Department of Health and Human Services, National Vital Statistics Reports, Volume 53, No. 9, November, 2004; p. 11, table 3; Volume 54, No. 8, December 29, 2005; p. 11, table 3.

NOTES: 'All mothers' includes mothers of other races and ethnic groups not shown separately. 'Asian' includes Asian or Pacific Islander. Data based on race of the mother.

UNITS: Total number of births, regardless of age of mother, per 1,000 women aged 15-44 years.

Table 9.03 Selected Characteristics of Live Births, 1980, 1990, 2000 and 2003

	Asian births	White births	All births
1980			
birth weight under 2,500 grams	6.68%	5.72%	6.84%
birth weight under 1,500 grams	0.92	0.90	1.15
mother under 18 years old	1.5	4.5	5.8
mother 18-19 years old	3.9	9.0	9.8
births to unmarried mothers	7.3	11.2	18.4
mother with less than 12 years of school	21.0	20.8	23.7
mother with 16 years or more of school	30.8	15.5	14.0
prenatal care began in 1st trimester	73.7	79.2	76.3
prenatal care began in 3rd trimester or no prenatal care	6.5	4.3	5.1
1990			
birth weight under 2,500 grams	6.45%	5.70%	6.97%
birth weight under 1,500 grams	0.87	0.95	1.27
mother under 18 years old	2.1	3.6	4.7
mother 18-19 years old	3.7	7.3	8.1
births to unmarried mothers	13.2	20.4	28.0
mother with less than 12 years of school	20.0	22.4	23.8
mother with 16 years or more of school	31.0	19.3	17.5
prenatal care began in 1st trimester	75.1	79.2	75.8
prenatal care began in 3rd trimester or no prenatal care	5.8	4.9	6.1

continued on the next page

Table 9.03 continued

	Asian births	White births	All births
2000			
birth weight under 2,500 grams	7.31%	6.55%	7.57%
birth weight under 1,500 grams	1.05	1.14	1.43
mother under 18 years old	1.5	3.5	4.1
mother 18-19 years old	3.0	7.1	7.7
births to unmarried mothers	14.8	27.1	33.2
mother with less than 12 years of school	11.6	21.4	21.7
mother with 16 years or more of school	42.8	26.3	24.7
prenatal care began in 1st trimester	84.0	85.0	83.2
prenatal care began in 3rd trimester or no prenatal care	3.3	3.3	3.9
2003			
birth weight under 2,500 grams	7.78%	6.94%	7.93%
birth weight under 1,500 grams	1.09	1.17	1.45
mother under 18 years old	51.1	3.0	3.4
mother 18-19 years old	2.4	6.4	6.9
births to unmarried mothers	15.0	29.4	34.6
mother with less than 12 years of school	9.9	21.8	21.6
mother with 16 years or more of school	47.1	27.9	26.6
prenatal care began in 1st trimester	85.4	85.7	84.1
prenatal care began in 3rd trimester or no prenatal care	3.1	3.0	3.5

SOURCE: U.S. Department of Health and Human Services, Health United States, 2005; p. 138, table 7; p. 141, table 9; p. 142, table 10; p. 143, table 11; p. 145, table 13. (Centers for Disease Control and Prevention, National Center for Health Statistics)

NOTES: Data based on race of the mother. 'Asian' includes 'Asian or Pacific Islander.' Prenatal care and maternal education data for 2003 exclude Pennsylvania and Washington that implemented the 2003 Revision to the U.S. Standard Certificate of Live Birth.

UNITS: Percent, as a percent of all live births, 100.0%.

Table 9.04 Projected Fertility Rates, Women 10-49 years old, 2010

	Asian women	White women	All women
2010			
Total fertility rate	2,252	2,098	2,123
birth rates			
10-14 years old	0.7	0.9	1.3
15-19 years old	29.6	54.3	60.2
20-24 years old	83.7	112.6	115.8
25-29 years old	134.5	118.5	115.7
30-34 years old	128.2	90.0	87.8
35-39 years old	59.0	36.6	36.7
40-44 years old	13.8	7.1	7.3
45-49 years old	0.9	0.3	0.3

SOURCE: U.S. Bureau of the Census, Statistical Abstract of the United States, 2006; p. 67, table 78 (data from U.S. Bureau of the Census, Population Division Working Paper No. 38).

NOTES: 'All Races' includes women of other races not shown separately. 'Asian' includes Asian or Pacific Islander. The total fertility rate is the number of births that 1,000 women would have in their lifetime if, at each year of age they experienced the birth rates occurring in the specified year. Projections are based on middle fertility assumptions.

UNITS: Total fertility rate and birth rate in births per 1,000 women.

Table 9.05 Health Status for Children, 2005

	Asian children	White children	All children
Respondent-assessed health status			
All children under 18	2,621	56,761	73,376
Excellent	1,284	31,809	39,979
Very good	874	15,599	20,302
Good	455	8,280	11,539
Fair/poor	†	1,068	1,540
Selected measures of health care access			
All children under 18	2804	56,561	73,374
Uninsured for health care	308	5,204	6,763
Unmet medical need	*42	1,170	1,513
Delayed care due to cost	*53	2,190	2,715

SOURCE: U.S. Department of Health and Human Services, Vital and Health Statistics, Series 10; Summary Health Statistics for U.S. Children: National Health Interview Survey, 2005; #231, Provisional Report, tables 5 and 15.

NOTES: 'All children' includes other races and ethnic groups not shown separately. '*' and '†'represent estimates that do not meet standard of reliability or precision.

UNITS: Number in thousands of children under 18 years of age.

Table 9.06 Vaccinations of Children 19-35 Months of Age for Selected Diseases, 2000 and 2004

	Asian	White	All Races
2000			
combined series (4:3:1:3)	75%	79%	76%
DTP (4 doses or more)	85	84	82
Polio (3 doses or more)	93	91	90
Measles-containing	90	92	91
Hib (3 doses or more)	92	95	93
Hepatitis B (3 doses or more)	91	91	90
Varicella	77	66	68
2004			
combined series (4:3:1:3)	84%	85%	83%
DTP (4 doses or more)	90	88	86
Polio (3 doses or more)	93	92	92
Measles-containing	94	94	93
Hib (3 doses or more)	92	95	94
Hepatitis B (3 doses or more)	93	93	92
Varicella	91	87	88

SOURCE: U.S. Department of Health and Human Services, Health United States, 2005, pp. 286-287, table 77 (Data from the National Immunization Survey, Centers for Disease Control and Prevention, National Center for Health Statistics).

NOTES: 'All Races' includes other races/ethnic groups not shown separately. 'White' excludes White Hispanics. Data excludes cases of residents of U.S. Territories. The 4:3:1:3 combined series consists of 4 doses of diphtheria-tetanus-pertussis (DTP) vaccine, 3 doses of polio vaccine, 1 dose of a measles-containing vaccine, and 3 doses of Haemophilus influenza type b (Hib) vaccine. DPT is the Diphtheria-tetanus-pertussis vaccine. Hib is the Haemophilus influenza type b (Hib) vaccine.

UNITS: Percent of children 19-35 months of age.

Table 9.07 Death Rates, by Age and Sex, 2004

	Asian		White		All Races	
	male	female	male	female	male	female
2004 (preliminary)						
All ages	318.6	276.1	854.3	874.6	816.4	817.0
under 1 year old	462.9	398.5	634.5	511.1	752.4	610.0
1-4 years old	20.2	20.1	29.1	25.0	32.2	27.7
5-14 years old	13.9	8.5	17.6	12.9	18.9	14.2
15-24 years old	53.4	23.3	107.2	42.2	113.2	43.2
25-34 years old	49.5	27.2	124.9	56.1	137.2	62.7
35-44 years old	87.6	52.9	225.6	128.6	239.9	142.4
45-54 years old	229.0	137.8	500.6	283.4	539.1	311.1
55-64 years old	528.3	335.3	1,061.0	670.6	1,121.2	705.9
65-74 years old	1,362.7	942.3	2,589.4	1,725.4	2,647.0	1,761.3
75-84 years old	3,766.3	2,670.7	6,406.2	4,535.8	6,408.6	4,538.8
85 years old and over	10,341.4	8,400.3	15,322.2	13,530.5	15,099.7	13,354.5

SOURCE: 2004: U.S. Department of Health and Human Services, Centers for Disease Control and Prevention, National Center for Health Statistics; National Vital Statistics Reports, Volume 54, No. 19, June 28, 2006; pp. 8-15, table 1.

NOTES: 'All Races' includes other races not shown separately. 'Asian' includes Asian or Pacific Islander. 'All Ages' includes ages not stated.

UNITS: Rates per 100,000 of population in specified age groups, as shown.

Table 9.08 Infant Mortality Rates, 1995 and 2000 - 2002

	Asian mothers	White mothers	All mothers
1995			
infant	5.3	6.3	7.6
neonatal	3.4	4.1	4.9
postneonatal	1.9	2.2	2.6
2000			
infant	4.9	5.7	6.9
neonatal	6.4	3.8	4.6
postneonatal	1.4	1.9	2.3
2001			
infant	4.7	5.7	6.8
neonatal	3.1	3.8	4.5
postneonatal	1.6	1.9	2.3
2002			
infant	4.8	5.8	7.0
neonatal	3.4	3.9	4.7
postneonatal	1.4	1.9	2.3

SOURCE: U.S. Department of Health and Human Services, Health United States, 2005, p. 214, table 43.

NOTES: Data based on race of mother. 'All Mothers' include mothers of other races not show separately. 'Asian' includes Asian or Pacific Islander. 'Infant' is under 1 year of age; 'neonatal' is under 28 days; 'postneonatal' is 28 days to 11 months.

UNITS: Number of deaths per 1,000 live births.

Table 9.09 Maternal Mortality Rates, 1980, 1990 and 2000 - 2003

	Asian mothers	White mothers	All mothers
1980	11	193	334
1990	9	177	343
2000	13	240	396
2001	16	228	399
2002	19	190	357
2003	25	280	495

SOURCE: U.S. Department of Health and Human Services, Health United States, 2005, p. 214, table 43.

NOTES: 'All Mothers' include mothers of other races not show separately. 'Asian' includes Asian or Pacific Islander. Data for maternal mortality for complications of pregnancy, childbirth and the puerperium. 2003 increases are due to methodological changes in reporting and data processing.

UNITS: Number of deaths of mothers per 100,000 live births.

Table 9.10 Deaths, by Top Ten Leading Causes, by Sex, 1980 and 2003

	Asian		White		All Persons	
	male	female	male	female	male	female
1980†						
Diseases of heart	2,174	1,091	364,679	318,668	405,661	355,424
Malignant neoplasms	1,485	1,037	198,188	169,974	225,948	190,561
Cerebrovascular diseases	521	507	60,095	88,639	69,973	100,252
Unintentional injuries	556	254	62,963	27,159	74,180	31,358
Chronic obstructive pulmonary diseases	158	*	35,977	16,398	38,625	17,425
Pneumonia and influenza	227	115	23,810	24,559	27,574	27,045
Diabetes mellitus	103	124	12,125	16,743	14,325	20,526
Chronic liver disease and cirrhosis	*	*	16,407	8,833	19,768	10,815
Atherosclerosis	*	*	10,543	16,526	*	17,848
Suicide	159	90	18,901	*	20,505	*
Homicide	151	60	*	*	18,779	*
Conditions originating in the perinatal period	128	118	*	6,512	*	9,815
Congenital anomolies	*	104	*	*	*	*

continued on the next page

Table 9.10 continued

	Asian		White		All Persons	
	male	female	male	female	male	female
2003††						
Diseases of heart	5,540	4,623	291,560	303,282	336,095	348,994
Malignant neoplasms	5,403	5,129	249,053	232,503	287,990	268,912
Cerebrovascular diseases	1,672	1,954	51,646	83,059	61,426	96,263
Chronic lower respiratory diseases	801	443	55,397	61,520	60,714	65,668
Unintentional injuries	1,192	780	59,912	33,469	70,532	38,745
Diabetes mellitus	707	738	28,939	30,160	35,438	38,781
Influenza and pneumonia	679	577	25,009	32,636	28,778	36,385
Alzheimer's disease	*	293	17,086	42,098	18,335	45,122
Nephritis, nephritic syndrome and nephrosis	304	332	16,408	17,299	20,481	21,972
Septicemia	*	*	*	15,271	*	19,082
Suicide	511	*	22,830	*	25,203	*
Homicide	287	*	*	*	*	*
Essential hypertension and hypertensive renal disease	*	265	*	*	*	*

SOURCE: U.S. Department of Health and Human Services, Health United States, 2005; pp. 178-181, table 31. (data from Centers for Disease Control and Prevention, National Center for Health Statistics, National Vital Statistics System; Vital Statistics of the United States, vol II, mortality, part A, 1980. Washington: Public Health Service. 1985; 2003 annual mortality file.)

NOTES: 'All Persons' includes other races not shown separately. 'Asian' includes Asian or Pacific Islander. The first ten causes of death listed are in rank order for all persons, both sexes. '*' – not a top ten cause of death for this group. '†' – cause of death is coded according to the Ninth Revision of the International Classification of Diseases (ICD-9).; '††' – cause of death is coded according to the Tenth Revision (ICD-10).

UNITS: Number of deaths.

Table 9.11 Death Rates for Malignant Neoplasms of the Breast, for Females, by Age, 1990 and 2003

	Asian women	White women	All women
1990			
All ages, age adjusted rate	13.7	33.2	33.3
All ages, crude rate	9.3	35.9	34.0
35-44 years old	8.4	17.1	17.8
45-54 years old	26.4	44.3	45.4
55-64 years old	33.8	78.5	78.6
65-74 years old	38.5	113.3	111.7
75-84 years old	48.0	148.2	146.3
85 years old and over	*na	198.0	196.8
2003			
All ages, age adjusted rate	12.6	24.7	25.3
All ages, crude rate	11.0	29.3	28.2
35-44 years old	7.6	11.1	12.2
45-54 years old	20.1	28.4	30.4
55-64 years old	33.8	54.9	56.6
65-74 years old	40.7	82.6	82.6
75-84 years old	41.4	124.6	123.7
85 years old and over	64.7	189.4	189.4

SOURCE: U.S. Department of Health and Human Services, Health United States, 2005 (Centers for Disease Control and Prevention, National Center for Health Statistics); pp. 206-207, table 40.

NOTES: 'All Women' includes women of other races/ethnic groups not shown separately. 'Asian' includes Asian or Pacific Islander. Data excludes deaths of nonresidents of the United States. *Indicates data based on fewer than 20 deaths. Age-adjusted rates for all years differ from those shown in previous editions of Health, United States. Age-adjusted rates are calculated using the year 2000 standard population starting with Health, United States, 2001.

UNITS: Rate is the number of deaths per 100,000 resident female population, by age group.

Table 9.12 Death Rates for Motor Vehicle Accidents, by Sex and Age, 2000 and 2003

	Asian		White		All Races	
	male	female	male	female	male	female
2000						
All ages, age adjusted	10.6	6.7	21.8	9.8	21.7	9.5
All ages, crude	9.8	5.9	21.6	10.0	21.3	9.7
1-14 years old	2.5	2.3	4.8	3.7	4.9	3.7
15-24 years old	17.0	6.0	39.6	17.1	37.4	15.9
25-34 years old	10.4	4.5	25.1	8.9	25.5	8.8
35-44 years old	6.9	4.9	21.8	8.9	22.0	8.8
45-64 years old	10.1	6.4	19.7	8.7	20.2	8.7
65 years old and over	21.1	18.5	29.4	16.2	29.5	15.8
2003						
All ages, age adjusted	10.3	6.8	21.9	9.5	21.6	9.3
All ages, crude	9.4	6.4	22.0	9.8	21.4	9.5
1-14 years old	2.4	1.7	4.7	3.2	4.7	3.3
15-24 years old	18.3	9.7	39.2	17.2	36.9	15.8
25-34 years old	8.2	4.5	25.9	8.6	25.5	8.5
35-44 years old	6.8	4.5	22.6	9.0	22.5	8.9
45-64 years old	9.7	7.5	20.6	8.5	20.9	8.6
65 years old and over	20.1	16.2	28.8	15.8	28.5	15.6

SOURCE: U.S. Department of Health and Human Services, Health, United States, 2005, (Centers for Disease Control and Prevention, National Center for Health Statistics) pp. 215-218, table 44.

NOTES: 'All Races' includes other races and ethnic groups not shown separately. 'Asian' includes Asian or Pacific Islander. Death rates for Asian or Pacific Islander populations are known to be underestimated. Excludes deaths of nonresidents of the United States. Age-adjusted rates for all years differ from those shown in previous editions of Health, United States. Age-adjusted rates are calculated using the year 2000 standard population starting with Health, United States, 2001.

UNITS: Rate is the number of deaths per 100,000 resident population.

Table 9.13 Death Rates for Assault (Homicide), by Sex and Age, 2000 and 2003

	Asian		White		All Races	
	male	female	male	female	male	female
2000						
All ages, age adjusted	4.3	1.7	5.2	2.1	9.0	2.8
All ages, crude	4.4	1.7	5.2	2.1	9.3	2.8
15-24 years old	7.8	*	9.9	2.7	20.9	3.9
25-44 years old	4.6	2.2	7.4	2.9	13.3	4.0
45-64 years old	6.1	2.0	4.1	1.8	6.0	2.1
2003						
All ages, age adjusted	4.2	1.6	5.3	2.0	9.4	2.6
All ages, crude	4.5	1.6	5.4	2.0	9.7	2.6
15-24 years old	9.8	*	10.6	2.5	21.8	3.7
25-44 years old	4.5	1.9	7.7	2.8	14.3	3.8
45-64 years old	4.3	1.5	4.2	1.8	6.1	2.1

SOURCE: U.S. Department of Health and Human Services, Health, United States, 2005, (Centers for Disease Control and Prevention, National Center for health Statistics), pp. 218-220, table 45.

NOTES: 'All Races' includes other races/ethnic groups not shown separately. 'Asian' includes Asian or Pacific Islander. Death rates for the Asian or Pacific Islander populations are known to be underestimated. Excludes deaths of nonresidents of the United States. *Based on fewer than 20 deaths. Age-adjusted rates for all years differ from those shown in previous editions of Health, United States. Age-adjusted rates are calculated using the year 2000 standard population starting with Health, United States, 2001.

UNITS: Rate is the number of deaths per 100,000 resident population

Table 9.14 Death Rates for Suicide, by Sex and Age, 2000 and 2003

	Asian		White		All Races	
	male	female	male	female	male	female
2000						
All ages, age adjusted	8.6	2.8	19.1	4.3	17.7	4.0
All ages, crude	7.9	2.7	18.8	4.4	17.1	4.0
15-24 years old	9.1	2.7	17.9	3.1	17.1	3.0
25-44 years old	9.9	3.3	22.9	6.0	21.3	5.4
45-64 years old	9.7	3.2	23.2	6.9	21.3	6.2
65 years old and over	15.4	5.2	33.3	4.3	31.1	4.0
2003						
All ages, age adjusted	8.5	3.1	19.6	4.6	18.0	4.2
All ages, crude	8.0	3.1	19.5	4.7	17.6	4.3
15-24 years old	9.0	3.4	16.9	3.1	16.0	3.0
25-44 years old	9.2	3.4	23.9	6.4	21.9	5.7
45-64 years old	10.0	4.3	26.1	7.8	23.5	7.0
65 years old and over	17.5	4.6	32.1	4.0	29.8	3.8

SOURCE: U.S. Department of Health and Human Services, Health United States, 2005 (Centers for Disease Control and Prevention, National Center for Health Statistics), pp. 221-223, table 46.

NOTES: 'All Races' includes other races and ethnic groups not shown separately. 'Asian' includes Asian or Pacific Islander. Death rates for the Asian or Pacific Islander populations are known to be underestimated. Excludes deaths of nonresidents of the United States. Age-adjusted rates for all years differ from those shown in previous editions of Health, United States. Age-adjusted rates are calculated using the year 2000 standard population starting with Health, United States, 2001.

UNITS: Rate is the number of deaths per 100,000 resident population.

Table 9.15 Death rates for Human Immunodeficiency Virus (HIV) infection, by Sex, 1987 - 2003

	Asian		White		All Races	
	male	female	male	female	male	female
1987	2.5	na	8.7	0.6	10.4	1.1
1990	4.3	na	15.7	1.1	18.5	2.2
1995	6.0	0.6	20.4	2.5	27.3	5.3
2000	1.2	0.2	4.6	1.0	7.9	2.5
2001	1.2	na	4.4	0.9	7.5	2.5
2002	1.5	na	4.3	0.9	7.4	2.5
2003	1.1	na	4.2	0.9	7.1	2.4

SOURCE: U.S. Department of Health and Human Services, Health United States, 2005, (Centers for Disease Control and Prevention, National Center for Health Statistics) pp. 211-212, table 42

NOTES: 'All Races' includes other races/ethnic groups not shown separately. 'Asian' includes Asian or Pacific Islander. Death rates for Asian or Pacific Islander populations are known to be underestimated. Age-adjusted rates for all years differ from those shown in previous editions of Health, United States. Age-adjusted rates are calculated using the year 2000 standard population starting with Health, United States, 2001.

UNITS: Number of deaths known to the Centers for Disease Control, by year of report.

Table 9.16 Persons 18 Years and Over With Selected Diseases and Conditions, 2003

	Asian	White	All Races
Total persons	7,361	177,830	213,042
diabetes	355	11,199	14,012
ulcers	256	12,513	14,456
kidney disease	72	2,420	3,017
liver disease	78	2,025	2,511
arthritis diagnosis	633	39,606	45,793
chronic joint symptoms	1,004	49,561	57,242

SOURCE: U.S. Census Bureau, Statistical Abstract of the United States: 2006; p. 127, table 184.

NOTES: 'All Races' includes other races not shown separately. 'Asian' and 'White' refers to persons who indicated only a single race group. A person may be represented in more than one column.

UNITS: Number in thousands of persons 18 years and over.

Table 9.17 AIDS (Acquired Immunodeficiency Syndrome) Cases, by Sex and Age, 1985 - 2003

	Asian	White	All Races
All years*			
children under 13 years old	57	1,613	8,939
persons over 13 years old			
male	5,875	333,873	708,452
female	905	33,766	156,837
1985			
children under 13 years old	0	26	131
persons over 13 years old			
male	47	4,746	7,504
female	1	143	524
1990			
children under 13 years old	4	157	725
persons over 13 years old			
male	254	20,825	36,179
female	20	1,228	4,544
1995			
children under 13 years old	5	117	745
persons over 13 years old			
male	463	26,028	56,689
female	69	3,042	12,978

continued on the next page

Table 9.17 continued

	Asian	White	All Races
2000			
children under 13 years old	3	32	189
persons over 13 years old			
male	275	11,314	30,135
female	71	1,859	9,958
2001			
children under 13 years old	3	30	170
persons over 13 years old			
male	325	11,054	30,663
female	164	1,993	10,617
2002			
children under 13 years old	4	23	150
persons over 13 years old			
male	351	11,221	31,644
female	67	1,930	10,951
2003			
children under 13 years old	1	23	153
persons over 13 years old			
male	458	11,831	32,781
female	105	1,923	11,297

SOURCE: U.S. Department of Health and Human Services, Health United States, 2004, p. 208, table 52 (data from Centers for Disease Control and Prevention, National Center for HIV, STD, and TB Prevention, Division of HIV/AIDS). HE 20.6223: (year)

NOTES: 'All Races' includes other races/ethnic groups not shown separately. 'White' excludes white Hispanics. Data excludes residents of U.S. Territories. Historic data is revised continually on an ongoing basis. Data for all years have been updated through June 30, 1999. * 'all years' includes cases prior to 1985. Data for all years have been updated through June 30, 2000, to include temporarily delayed case reports and may differ from previous editions of Health, United States.

UNITS: Number of cases known to the Centers for Disease Control, by year of report; percent distribution as a percent of total (100.0%).

Table 9.18 Cancer Incidence Rates, Selected Cancer Sites, by Sex, 1990, 2000 and 2002

	Asian		White		All Races	
	male	female	male	female	male	female
1990						
All sites	387.6	294.9	590.9	421.3	584.2	411.3
lung/bronchus	64.3	28.4	94.4	48.6	95.1	47.3
colon/rectum	61.4	38.3	73.0	49.7	72.3	50.2
oral cavity/pharynx	14.9	6.0	18.0	7.4	18.5	7.3
stomach	26.9	15.5	12.8	5.7	14.6	6.7
pancreas	11.2	9.9	12.7	9.8	13.1	10.0
urinary bladder	15.6	5.3	40.7	9.9	37.2	9.5
non-Hodgkin's lymphoma	16.5	9.0	23.7	15.4	22.7	14.5
leukemia	8.5	6.1	17.9	10.2	17.1	9.8
prostate	88.8	na	168.2	na	166.7	na
breast	na	86.9	na	134.3	na	129.2
cervix uteri	na	12.1	na	11.3	na	11.9
corpus uteri	na	13.3	na	26.4	na	24.7
ovary	na	11.1	na	16.4	na	15.5
2000						
All sites	387.3	292.9	561.2	426.9	557.3	409.7
lung/bronchus	62.8	27.1	75.9	50.6	77.2	48.4
colon/rectum	56.3	36.5	61.9	45.4	62.2	45.8
oral cavity/pharynx	12.9	6.2	15.6	6.2	15.7	6.2
stomach	22.1	12.8	10.6	5.0	12.5	6.1
pancreas	10.4	9.0	12.5	9.6	12.7	9.8
urinary bladder	16.4	4.1	40.5	9.8	36.5	9.0
non-Hodgkin's lymphoma	15.8	11.1	24.6	16.6	23.2	15.7
leukemia	9.8	6.1	16.7	10.4	15.8	9.8
prostate	104.4	na	171.1	na	175.9	na
breast	na	91.6	na	140.1	na	133.1
cervix uteri	na	8.0	na	8.8	na	8.8
corpus uteri	na	16.2	na	25.5	na	23.8
ovary	na	9.8	na	14.9	na	14.0

continued on the next page

Table 9.18 continued

	Asian		White		All Races	
	male	female	male	female	male	female
2002						
All sites	375.4	308.1	539.4	418.2	537.2	404.4
lung/bronchus	55.5	28.4	72.5	49.9	73.3	47.7
colon/rectum	57.0	40.7	57.4	43.2	58.5	44.2
oral cavity/pharynx	12.6	5.8	15.3	6.4	15.3	6.3
stomach	20.0	10.8	10.2	4.9	11.8	6.0
pancreas	9.4	8.7	12.5	9.6	12.2	10.0
urinary bladder	19.5	3.1	37.9	10.0	34.6	9.0
non-Hodgkin's lymphoma	16.3	11.5	23.9	16.7	22.9	15.8
leukemia	8.9	6.0	15.9	9.3	14.9	8.8
prostate	98.7	na	166.3	na	171.5	na
breast	na	97.4	na	135.8	na	129.9
cervix uteri	na	8.1	na	8.1	na	8.2
corpus uteri	na	18.6	na	24.4	na	23.6
ovary	na	11.6	na	14.0	na	13.3

SOURCE: U.S. Department of Health and Human Services, Health United States, 2005; table 53. (Data from Surveillance, Epidemiology, and End Results (SEER) Program's 13 population-based cancer registries, November 2004 submission.)

NOTES: 'All Races' includes other races not shown separately. 'Asian' includes Asian or Pacific Islander.

UNITS: Number of new cases per 100,000 population.

Table 9.19 Medical Injury or Poisoning Episodes, 2004

	Asian	White	All Races
2004			
all persons	10,955	234,601	288,252
all episodes	657	27,975	31,173
fall	*200	10,524	12,030
struck by person or object	†	3,293	3,852
transportation	†	2,843	3,690
over-exertion	†	3,987	4,763
cutting / piercing instrument	†	2,516	2,844
other causes	†	4,551	5,619
poisoning	†	*261	375

SOURCE: U.S. Department of Health and Human Services, Vital and Health Statistics, Series 10; #229 (2006), tables 8 and 9 (data from the National Health Interview Survey, 2004)

NOTES: 'All Races' includes other races not shown separately. Based on a question in survey that asked all respondents whether they had been poisoned and/or injured seriously enough in the past 3 months to seek medical advice or treatment. '*' and '†'represent estimates that do not meet standard of reliability or precision.

UNITS: Number of persons or incidents in thousands.

Table 9.20 Limitation of Activity, 2004

	Asian	White	All Races
2004			
Physical activities that are very difficult or cannot be done at all			
any physical difficulty	8.2%	14.5%	14.7%
walk a quarter of a mile	2.9	6.7	7.0
climb up to 10 steps without resting	2.4	5.0	5.3
stand for 2 hours	5.4	8.3	8.6
sit for 2 hours	*2.0	3.1	3.1
stoop, bend or kneel	3.9	8.4	8.5
reach over one's head	*1.1	2.4	2.4
grasp or handle small objects	*1.3	1.8	1.8
lift or carry 10 pounds	4.8	4.0	4.3
push or pull large objects	4.7	6.3	6.5

SOURCE: U.S. Department of Health and Human Services, Vital and Health Statistics, Series 10; #228, table 19 (data from the National Health Interview Survey).

NOTES: 'All Races' includes other races not shown separately. '*' represents estimates that do not meet standard of reliability or precision.

UNITS: Percent as a percent of the population of 18 years of age and over.

Table 9.21 Work-Loss Days, 2004

	Asian	White	All Races
2004			
All persons	7,853	178,552	215,191
bed days in the past 12 months	14,063	728,668	872,431
days per person	1.8	4.1	4.1
All employed persons	5,827	125,757	151,650
work-loss days in the past 12 months	12,568	476,176	578,319
days per person	2.2	3.8	3.9

SOURCE: U.S. Department of Health and Human Services, Vital and Health Statistics, Series 10; #228 (2006), table 17 (data from the National Health Interview Survey).

NOTES: 'All Races' includes other races not shown separately. Respondents were asked how many times in the last 12 months an injury or illness caused them to miss a day of work or had kept them in bed more than half a day.

UNITS: Number of work-loss days per 100 persons 18 years old and over, currently employed.

Table 9.22 Self-Assessment of Health, 1995, 2000 and 2003

	Asian*	White	All Races
Self-assessment of health			
1995			
fair or poor	9.3%	9.7%	10.6%
2000			
fair or poor	7.4%	8.2%	9.0%
2003			
fair or poor	7.4%	8.5%	9.2%

SOURCE: U.S. Department of Health and Human Services, Health, United States, 2005, p. 248, table 60 (Centers for Disease Control and Prevention, National Center for Health Statistics, National Health Interview Survey).

NOTES: 'All Races' includes other races not shown separately. Data **are** age-adjusted. Data starting in 1997 are not strictly comparable with data for earlier years due to the 1997 questionnaire redesign. * Asian only. Prior to 1999, 'Asian only' included Native Hawaiian and Other Pacific Islander.

UNITS: Percent of the population.

Table 9.23 Use of Selected Substances by Persons 12 Years Old and Older, 2002 and 2003

	Asian	White	All Races
2002			
any illicit drug	3.5%	8.5%	8.3%
marijuana	1.8	6.5	6.2
psychotherapeutic drug*	0.7	2.8	2.6
alcohol	37.1	55.0	51.0
binge alcohol	12.4	23.4	22.9
any tobacco	18.6	32.0	30.4
cigarettes	17.7	26.9	26.0
cigars	1.1	5.5	5.4
2003			
any illicit drug	3.8%	8.3%	8.2%
marijuana	1.9	6.4	6.2
psychotherapeutic drug*	1.7	2.8	2.7
alcohol	39.8	54.4	50.1
binge alcohol	11.0	23.6	22.6
any tobacco	13.8	31.6	29.8
cigarettes	12.6	26.6	25.4
cigars	1.8	5.4	5.4

SOURCE: U.S. Department of Health and Human Services, Health United States, 2005, pp.259-260, table 66.

NOTES: 'All Races' includes other races not shown separately. 'Asian' and 'White' exclude Hispanic persons. Use of selected substances in the past month by person 12 years of age and over.

Any illicit drug includes marijuana/hashish, cocaine, heroin, hallucinogens, or any psychotherapeutic drug for nonmedical use.

*Psychotherapeutic drug for nonmedical use includes prescription-type pain relievers, tranquilizers, stimulants, or sedatives; does not include over-the-counter drugs.

Binge Alcohol: Five or more drinks on the same occasion at least once in the past month.

UNITS: Percent as a percent of population by selected substance.

Table 9.24 Health Care Visits, 2003

	Asian	White	All Races
2003			
Number of health care visits*			
none	22.6%	15.7%	15.8%
1-3 visits	47.8	45.6	45.8
4-9 visits	20.7	25.1	24.8
10 or more visits	8.9	13.6	13.6

SOURCE: U.S. Department of Health and Human Services, Health United States, 2005; pp. 281-283, table 75

NOTES: *`Health care visits" include ambulatory and home health care visits during a 12-month period.

UNITS: Number of visits per 100 persons

Table 9.25 Use of Pap smears, Women 18 Years and Over, 1999, 2000 and 2003

	Asian women	White women	All women
1999	64.4%	80.6%	80.8%
2000	66.4	81.3	81.2
2003	68.3	78.7	79.0

SOURCE: U.S. Department of Health and Human Services, Health, United States, 2005, p. 307, table 87.

NOTES: 'All women' includes other races not shown separately. Data not age-adjusted.

UNITS: Percent of women 18 years of age and over.

Table 9.26 Use of Mammography, Women 40 Years and Over, 1990 - 2003

	Asian women	White women	All women
1999	58.3%	70.6%	70.3%
2000	53.5	71.4	70.4
2003	57.6	70.1	69.7

SOURCE: U.S. Department of Health and Human Services, Health, United States, 2005, p. 305, table 86.

NOTES: 'All women' includes other races not shown separately. Data not age-adjusted.

UNITS: Percent of women 40 years of age and over.

Table 9.27 Short Stay Hospitals: Discharges, Days of Care, Average Length of Stay, 2002-2003

	Asian	White	All Races
2002			
discharges	45.0	96.4	122.9
days of care	*	343.0	541.0
average length of stay	*	3.6	4.4
2003			
discharges	53.2	93.2	119.9
days of care	*	378.3	558.9
average length of stay	*	4.1	4.7

SOURCE: U.S. Department of Health and Human Services, Health United States, (Centers for Disease Control and Prevention, National Center for Health Statistics; data from the National Health Interview Survey); 2005; p. 324, table 96.

NOTES: 'All Races' includes other races not shown separately. Data **are** age adjusted. * indicates data have a relative standard error of greater than 30%.

UNITS: Discharges and days of care in number per 1,000 population; average length of stay, in average number of days.

Table 9.28 Health Care Coverage for Persons Under 65 Years of Age, by Type of Coverage, 1995 and 2000 - 2003

	Asian	White	All Races
1995			
Private insurance	68.4%	74.5%	71.3%
Private insurance obtained through workplace	59.6	68.4	65.4
Medicaid or other public assistance	10.5	8.9	11.5
not covered	18.6	15.5	16.1
2000			
Private insurance	72.1%	75.7%	71.5%
Private insurance obtained through workplace	65.1	70.6	66.7
Medicaid or other public assistance	7.5	7.1	9.5
not covered	17.6	15.4	17.0
2001			
Private insurance	72.3%	75.1%	71.2%
Private insurance obtained through workplace	65.9	70.2	66.7
Medicaid or other public assistance	8.4	8.0	10.4
not covered	17.3	14.9	16.4
2002			
Private insurance	70.9%	73.4%	69.4%
Private insurance obtained through workplace	62.5	68.7	65.0
Medicaid or other public assistance	9.8	9.3	11.8
not covered	17.4	15.5	16.8
2003			
Private insurance	71.4%	71.5%	68.9%
Private insurance obtained through workplace	62.1	65.6	63.3
Medicaid or other public assistance	8.0	10.4	12.3
not covered	18.2	16.0	16.5

SOURCE: U.S. Department of Health and Human Services, Health United States, 2005; pp. 379-381, table 132; pp. 382-383, table 133; pp. 384-385, table 134.

NOTES: 'All Races' includes other races not shown separately. Medicaid includes persons receiving AFDC (Aid to Families with Dependent Children) or SSI (Supplemental Security Income), or those with a current Medicaid card. Not covered includes those persons not covered by private insurance, Medicaid, Medicare, and military plans. Data **are** age-adjusted. The questionnaire changed in 1997 compared with previous years.

UNITS: Percent of the population.

Table 9.29 Health Care Coverage for Persons 65 Years of Age and Over, by Type of Coverage, 1995, 2000 and 2003

	Asian	White	All Races
1995			
Private insurance	45.8%	78.3%	74.6%
Private insurance obtained through workplace	27.0	41.0	39.5
Medicaid or other public assistance	33.6	7.2	9.4
Medicare HMO	na	na	na
2000			
Private insurance	42.9%	67.2%	63.4%
Private insurance obtained through workplace	25.0	37.4	35.9
Medicaid or other public assistance	21.0	5.5	7.5
Medicare HMO	16.7	15.1	15.2
2003			
Private insurance	40.2%	65.7%	62.7%
Private insurance obtained through workplace	25.9	35.7	34.8
Medicaid or other public assistance	28.5	6.2	8.0
Medicare HMO	15.2	10.0	10.0

SOURCE: U.S. Department of Health and Human Services, Health United States, 2005, (Centers for Disease Control and Prevention, National Center for Health Statistics) pp. 386-.88, table 135.

NOTES: 'All Races' includes other races not shown separately. Medicaid includes public assistance through 1996; includes state-sponsored health plans starting with 1997. Data **are** age-adjusted. The questionnaire changed in 1997 compared with previous years.

UNITS: Percent of the population.

Table 9.30 Health Insurance Coverage, 2002 - 2004

	Asian	White	All Races
Not covered by private or government health insurance			
total, 2002	18.4%	14.2%	15.2%
children under 18 years	na	11.1	11.6
total, 2003	18.8%	14.6%	15.6%
children under 18 years	12.4	7.4	11.4
total, 2004	16.8%	14.9%	15.7%
children under 18 years	9.4	7.6	11.2

SOURCE: U.S. Bureau of the Census, Current Population Reports: Income, Poverty, and Health Insurance Coverage in the United States: 2003; Series P-60, #226; p. 15, table 5; p.19, figure 7; issued August 2004; 2004; Series P-60, #229; p. 18, table 7; p. 21, figure 7; issued August 2005.

NOTES: 'All Races' includes other races and ethnic groups not shown separately. 'White' as shown is equivalent to 'White Alone' that refers to people who reported 'White' and did not report any other race category.

UNITS: Percent as a percent of all persons in households, 100.0%.

Chapter 10: Special Topics

Table 10.01 Selected Characteristics of Farms and Farm Operators, 2002

	Asian farms	All farms
Characteristics of farms		
Farms and land in farms		
farms (number)	8,375	2,128,982
land in farms (acres)	990,317	938,279,056
harvested cropland (acres)	na	302,697,252
Farms by size		
1-9 acres	3,033	179,346
10-49 acres	2,862	563,772
50-179 acres	1,500	658,705
180-499 acres	601	388,617
500 acres or more	379	338,542
Owned and rented land in farms		
owned land in farms		
farms	6,816	1,979,140
acres	643,113	584,963,623
rented or leased land in farms		
farms	2,440	700,846
acres	347,204	353,315,433
2002 Market value of agricultural products sold, (in thousands of dollars)		
total	$2,261,692	$200,646,355
average per farm	na	94,245
crops (including nursery and greenhouse crops)	2,007,907	95,151,954
livestock, poultry and their products	253,785	105,494,401
Farms by value of sales		
less than $1,000	907	430,953
$1,000-$2,499	794	307,368
$2,500-$4,999	605	243,026
$5,000-$9,999	838	246,624
$10,000-$24,999	1,194	272,333
$25,000-$49,999	858	163,521
$50,000 or more	3,179	465,157

continued on the next page

Table 10.01 continued

	Asian farms	All farms
Farms by North American Industry Classification System		
oilseed and grain farming (1111)	209	37,540,988
vegetable and melon farming (11112)	1,203	13,145,448
fruit and tree nut farming (1113)	3,422	13,489,154
greenhouse, nursery, and floriculture production (1114)	1,589	15,065,589
other crop farming (1119)	587	14,548,102
tobacco farming (11191)	8	1,506,953
cotton farming (11192)	17	3,789,565
sugarcane farming, hay farming, and all other crop farming (11193, 11194, 11199)	562	8,315,743
beef cattle ranching and farming (112111)	560	19,755,572
cattle feedlots (112112)	36	22,895,343
dairy cattle and milk production (11212)	31	22,737,525
hog and pig farming (1122)	75	12,337,959
poultry and egg production (1123)	265	24,410,930
sheep and goat farming (1124)	87	445,366
animal aquaculture and other animal production (1125, 1129)	311	4,274,380
Operator characteristics		
Total operators	13,089	2,128,982
Residence		
on farm operated	8,174	1,680,160
not on farm operated	4,915	448,822
Principal occupation		
farming	7,890	1,224,246
other	5,199	904,736
Days of work off farm		
none	6,795	962,200
any	6,294	1,166,782
1-49 days	1,030	122,248
50-99 days	561	66,306
100-199 days	889	145,880
200 days or more	3,814	832,348

continued on the next page

Table 10.01 continued

	Asian farms	All farms
Characteristics of the farm operator - continued		
Years on present farm		
2 years or less	868	74,754
3 or 4 years	1,328	143,599
5 to 9 years	3,171	374,756
10 years or more	7,722	1,535,873
average years on present farm	na	20.7
Age		
under 25 years old	231	16,962
25-34 years old	764	106,097
35-44 years old	2,561	366,306
45-54 years old	4,150	572,664
55-64 years old	2,689	509,123
65 years old and over	2,694	557,830
average age	53.0	55.3
Sex		
male	8,851	1,891,163
female	4,238	237,819
Principal operator is a hired manager		
farms	632	55,372
acres	153,087	103,135,293

SOURCE: U.S. Bureau of the Census, 2002 Census of Agriculture, Vol. 1 Geographic Area Series, Part 51, U.S. Summary and State Data; p. 8, table 2; p. 16, table 9; p. 52, table 50; pp. 214-226, table 61; pp. 48-29, table 47; pp. 54-55, table 52. C 3.31/4:002/v. 1/ pt. 51

NOTES: 'All farms' includes farms owned/operated by persons of all races.

UNITS: Farms, farms by size, farms by organization, farms by value of sales, farms by Standard Industrial Classification, in number of farms; land in farms and harvested crop lands in acres; market value of agricultural products sold in thousands of dollars. Characteristics of farm operators in number of farm operators.

Table 10.02 Farms and Operators, by State, 2002

	Asian			White		
	Farms	Operators	Land in Farms	Farms	Operators	Land in Farms
total	*10,300*	*13,089*	*1,448,061*	*2,077,656*	*2,966,230*	*883,755,206*
Alabama	49	51	3,183	42,407	57,863	8,613,879
Alaska	3	4	na	574	825	590,627
Arizona	62	70	25,654	6,950	11,110	4,846,435
Arkansas	93	121	10,884	45,834	65,838	14,241,472
California	4,022	5,379	529,162	75,166	112,321	26,791,340
Colorado	84	108	46,773	31,050	48,283	30,689,204
Connecticut	6	6	278	4,178	6,425	354,618
Delaware	27	29	809	2,345	3,537	535,686
District of Columbia	na	na	na	na	na	na
Florida	557	689	29,897	42,358	60,195	10,265,971
Georgia	99	124	8,057	47,161	63,239	10,468,416
Hawaii	2,286	2,969	157,235	2,367	3,149	1,046,617
Idaho	110	139	66,579	24,831	37,372	11,328,031
Illinois	36	38	17,736	72,863	99,430	27,284,004
Indiana	41	48	6,142	60,129	85,055	15,041,774
Iowa	57	64	10,437	90,544	124,932	31,708,937
Kansas	28	28	10,982	64,067	87,987	47,110,383
Kentucky	52	54	6,493	85,670	119,703	13,756,749
Louisiana	35	46	4,347	25,475	35,170	7,611,921
Maine	16	19	982	7,163	11,051	1,357,281
Maryland	39	49	1,505	11,893	17,740	2,058,069
Massachusetts	24	33	464	6,016	9,402	516,536
Michigan	64	76	4,418	52,977	77,320	10,111,573
Minnesota	84	100	7,719	80,694	111,794	27,472,772
Mississippi	50	52	9,411	37,104	50,069	10,500,522
Missouri	104	104	18,114	106,023	153,143	29,788,866
Montana	35	38	83,107	27,066	40,669	55,645,998
Nebraska	13	13	3,541	49,262	69,393	45,856,918
Nevada	12	12	4,190	2,896	4,605	5,170,392
New Hampshire	14	15	3,860	3,334	5,339	441,164
New Jersey	70	100	4,281	9,781	14,715	796,328
New Mexico	45	48	5,317	14,732	21,219	37,459,047

continued on the next page

Table 10.02 continued

	Asian			White		
	Farms	Operators	Land in Farms	Farms	Operators	Land in Farms
New York	82	89	8,577	37,026	55,896	7,637,736
North Carolina	117	152	8,062	51,705	71,052	8,830,220
North Dakota	5	5	5,676	30,418	40,761	38,782,289
Ohio	61	66	5,594	77,387	110,563	14,536,960
Oklahoma	106	116	14,105	78,451	108,877	32,453,807
Oregon	362	429	70,068	39,401	62,551	16,272,697
Pennsylvania	54	55	4,030	57,922	84,577	7,727,960
Rhode Island	na	na	na	857	1,263	60,873
South Carolina	32	35	4,578	22,592	30,303	4,647,856
South Dakota	22	22	23,401	31,177	43,728	40,846,450
Tennessee	107	126	7,811	86,268	118,922	11,556,118
Texas	440	500	130,153	221,687	317,543	128,788,032
Utah	52	59	5,262	15,174	22,850	7,416,128
Vermont	16	17	1,205	6,543	10,376	1,240,975
Virginia	96	109	9,502	45,906	65,793	8,403,996
Washington	385	493	41,304	35,268	53,209	12,827,510
West Virginia	15	18	na	20,750	28,946	3,574,692
Wisconsin	106	146	8,053	76,928	115,193	15,717,963
Wyoming	25	26	17,294	9,286	14,934	32,971,414

SOURCE: U.S. Bureau of the Census, 2002 Census of Agriculture, Vol. 1 Geographic Area Series, Part 51, U.S. Summary and State Data; p. 551, table 41; p. 555, table 45. C 3.31/4:002/v. 1/ pt. 51

NOTES: 'All farms' includes farms owned/operated by persons of all races.

UNITS: Farms, farms by size, farms by organization, farms by value of sales, farms by Standard Industrial Classification, in number of farms; land in farms and harvested crop lands in acres; market value of agricultural products sold in thousands of dollars. Characteristics of farm operators in number of farm operators.

Table 10.03 Minority-Owned Businesses, 1997

	Asian	All Minorities	All Firms U.S.
1997			
all firms	912,960	3,039,033	20,821,935
sales & receipts	$306,932,982	$591,259,123	$18,553,243,047
firms with paid employees	289,999	615,222	5,295,152
sales & receipts	$278,294,345	$516,979,920	$17,907,940,321
employees	2,203,079	4,514,699	103,359,815
annual payroll	$46,179,519	$95,528,782	$2,936,492,940

SOURCE: U.S. Bureau of the Census, 1997 Economic Censuses Survey of Minority-Owned Business Enterprises; printed from www.census.gov/epcd/mwb97/us/us.html on July 14, 2006.

NOTES: Data from the 1997 Economic Census. 'Asian' as shown is equivalent to 'Asian and Pacific Islander'.

UNITS: Firms in number of firms; sales and receipts in thousands of dollars; employees in number of employees; annual payroll in thousands of dollars

Table 10.04 Asian-Owned Firms, by Ethnic Group, 1997

	all firms		firms with paid employees			
	firms	sales & receipts	firms	sales & receipts	employees	annual payroll
1997						
Asian	912,960	$306,932,982	289,999	$278,294,345	2,203,079	$46,179,519
Asian Indian	166,737	67,503,357	67,189	61,760,453	490,629	12,585,621
Chinese	252,577	106,196,794	90,582	98,233,262	691,757	12,944,824
Filipino	84,534	11,077,885	14,581	8,966,386	110,130	2,667,333
Japanese	85,538	43,741,051	23,309	41,294,865	262,223	7,106,692
Korean	135,571	45,936,497	50,076	40,745,504	333,649	5,789,472
Vietnamese	97,764	9,322,891	18,948	6,768,324	79,035	1,165,550
Other Asian	70,868	19,016,149	22,292	16,800,603	201,610	3,135,784
Hawaiian	15,544	2,250,153	2,023	1,956,793	20,698	497,950
Other Pacific Islander	3,826	1,888,205	1,000	1,768,155	13,349	286,293

SOURCE: U.S. Bureau of the Census, 1997 Economic Censuses Survey of Minority-Owned Business Enterprises; printed from www.census.gov/epcd/mwb97/us/us.html on July 14, 2006.

NOTES: Data from the 1997 Economic Census. 'Asian' as shown is equivalent to 'Asian and Pacific Islander'.

UNITS: Firms in number of firms; sales and receipts in thousands of dollars; employees in number of employees; annual payroll in thousands of dollars

Table 10.05 Asian-Owned Firms, by Major Industry Group, 1997

	all firms		firms with paid employees			
	firms	sales & receipts	firms	sales & receipts	employees	annual payroll
1997						
All industries	912,960	$306,932,982	289,999	$278,294,345	2,203,079	$46,179,519
agricultural services, forestry and fishing	12,988	1,140,670	1,927	791,843	11,359	226,707
mining	660	253,329	87	229,059	1,007	33,447
construction	27,711	7,485,505	6,398	6,522,807	42,533	1,386,303
manufacturing	23,242	28,952,417	10,553	28,271,707	238,167	5,513,875
transportation and public utilities	37,501	5,625,483	5,916	4,427,646	52,441	1,220,240
wholesale trade	50,400	105,466,223	30,095	102,902,082	211,510	6,128,070
retail trade	195,691	67,895,241	106,264	62,467,158	644,644	7,497,710
finance, insurance, and real estate	68,765	11,398,069	9,429	7,585,054	42,243	1,185,688
services	406,010	67,762,462	107,910	57,153,191	896,731	21,719,605
industries not classified	90,509	10,953,582	11,937	7,943,797	62,443	1,267,874

SOURCE: U.S. Bureau of the Census, 1997 Economic Censuses Survey of Minority-Owned Business Enterprises; printed from www.census.gov/epcd/mwb97/us/us.html on July 14, 2006.

NOTES: Data from the 1997 Economic Census. 'Asian' as shown is equivalent to 'Asian and Pacific Islander'.

UNITS: Firms in number of firms; sales and receipts in thousands of dollars; employees in number of employees; annual payroll in thousands of dollars

Table 10.06 Minority-Owned Businesses, 2002

	Asian	White	All Firms U.S.
2002			
all firms	1,105,329	19,894,823	22,977,164
sales & receipts	$343,321,501	$8,303,716,399	$22,634,870,406
firms with paid employees	319,911	4,712,168	5,526,111
sales & receipts	$307,555,836	$7,629,211,216	$21,867,386,411
employees	2,293,694	52,209,027	110,832,682
annual payroll	$58,624,239	$1,548,757,745	$3,815,069,400

SOURCE: U.S. Bureau of the Census, 2002 Economic Census Survey of Business Owners Preliminary Estimates of Business Ownership by Gender, Hispanic or Latino Origin, and Race:2002; issued July, 2005.
U.S. Bureau of the Census, 2002 Economic Census Survey of Business Owners: Asian-Owned Firms:2002; SB02-00CS-ASIAN, issued May 2006.

NOTES: Data from the 2002 Economic Census. 'Asian' as shown is equivalent to 'Asian Alone'. 'Native Hawaiian and Pacific Islander' is categorized separately.

UNITS: Firms in number of firms; sales and receipts in thousands of dollars; employees in number of employees; annual payroll in thousands of dollars

Table 10.07 Asian-Owned Firms, by Ethnic Group, 2002

	all firms		firms with paid employees			
	firms	sales & receipts	firms	sales & receipts	employees	annual payroll
2002						
Asian	1,104,189	$326,352,983	319,295	$290,805,663	2,212,813	$55,991,382
Asian Indian	231,179	89,022,573	83,522	80,786,633	615,549	17,655,262
Chinese	290,197	106,269,540	90,179	96,771,671	656,565	15,472,533
Filipino	128,223	14,614,862	20,149	11,306,707	133,933	3,642,822
Japanese	86,863	30,622,830	22,166	27,854,820	205,423	5,780,834
Korean	158,031	46,947,937	57,078	41,279,844	320,522	6,699,091
Vietnamese	147,081	15,651,008	25,636	11,671,482	127,785	2,816,459
Other Asian	71,439	20,315,711	21,443	18,353,035	138,634	3,239,646

SOURCE: U.S. Bureau of the Census, 2002 Economic Census Survey of Business Owners: Asian-Owned Firms; SB02-00CS-ASIAN, "(Table 1) Statistics for Asian-Owned Firms by Kind of Business and Detailed Group: 2002", issued May 2006.

NOTES: Data from the 2002 Economic Census. 'Asian' as shown is equivalent to 'Asian Alone'. 'Native Hawaiian and Pacific Islander' is categorized separately.

UNITS: Firms in number of firms; sales and receipts in thousands of dollars; employees in number of employees; annual payroll in thousands of dollars

Table 10.08 Asian-Owned Firms, by Receipts Size, 2002

	all firms		firms with paid employees			
	firms	sales & receipts	firms	sales & receipts	employees	annual payroll
2002						
Asian	1,104,189	$326,352,983	319,295	$290,805,663	2,212,813	$55,991,382
less than $5,000	175,260	437,430	2,461	5,967	16,945	638,479
$5,000 to $9,999	142,716	961,413	4,042	28,384	1,393	14,101
$10,000 to $24,999	199,977	3,129,322	11,931	201,424	7,092	64,808
$25,000 to $49,999	139,646	4,927,455	20,035	737,852	18,996	203,960
$50,000 to $99,999	121,566	8,653,649	37,658	2,784,997	55,767	715,846
$100,000 to $249,999	141,314	22,427,255	83,791	13,872,313	227,708	3,303,524
$250,000 to $499,999	82,051	28,969,200	65,242	23,243,972	303,353	5,558,495
$500,000 to $999,999	52,081	36,164,214	45,635	31,761,792	368,453	7,743,985
$1,000,000 or more	49,578	220,683,046	48,500	218,168,961	1,213,106	37,748,184

SOURCE: U.S. Bureau of the Census, 2002 Economic Census Survey of Business Owners: Asian-Owned Firms; SB02-00CS-ASIAN, "(Table 8) Statistics for Asian-Owned Firms by Kind of Business and Receipts Size of Firm: 2002", issued May 2006.

NOTES: Data from the 2002 Economic Census. 'Asian' as shown is equivalent to 'Asian Alone'. 'Native Hawaiian and Pacific Islander' is categorized separately.

UNITS: Firms in number of firms; sales and receipts in thousands of dollars; employees in number of employees; annual payroll in thousands of dollars

Table 10.09 Asian-Owned Firms, by Employment Size, 2002

	firms	receipts	employees	payroll
2002				
Asian	319,295	$290,805,663	2,212,813	$55,991,382
no employees	54,248	10,268,597	na	1,612,253
1 to 4 employees	160,671	56,958,184	346,666	7,943,633
5 to 9 employees	54,625	46,047,169	352,608	7,972,149
10 to 19 employees	29,702	44,105,702	392,938	9,124,290
20 to 49 employees	14,910	50,918,661	437,247	10,943,692
50 to 99 employees	3,277	30,759,075	226,238	6,047,778
100 to 499 employees	1,735	32,767,922	301,913	8,193,242
500 employees or more	128	18,980,352	155,204	4,154,345

SOURCE: U.S. Bureau of the Census, 2002 Economic Census Survey of Business Owners: Asian-Owned Firms; SB02-00CS-ASIAN, "(Table 9) Statistics for Asian-Owned Firms with Paid Employees by Kind of Business and Employment Size of Firm: 2002", issued May 2006.

NOTES: Data from the 2002 Economic Census. 'Asian' as shown is equivalent to 'Asian Alone'. 'Native Hawaiian and Pacific Islander' is categorized separately.

UNITS: Firms in number of firms; sales and receipts in thousands of dollars; employees in number of employees; annual payroll in thousands of dollars

Table 10.10 Asian-Owned Firms, by Major Industry Group, 2002

	all firms		firms with paid employees			
	firms	sales & receipts	firms	sales & receipts	employees	annual payroll
2002						
All industries	1,104,189	$326,352,983	319,295	$290,805,663	2,212,813	$55,991,382
agricultural services, forestry and fishing	6,261	490,646	224	237,379	1,147	43,828
mining	456	213,054	59	200,716	730	31,796
utilities	225	36,739	41	31,172	256	6,076
construction	38,742	9,720,210	7,397	8,135,150	46,927	1,666,045
manufacturing	23,716	26,445,057	11,844	25,934,628	169,879	5,115,700
wholesale trade	46,554	87,079,166	24,556	83,919,720	154,518	5,589,992
retail trade	151,551	64,930,753	61,622	58,351,545	291,351	4,988,552
transportation and warehousing	52,046	4,961,360	3,321	3,204,587	25,050	677,931
information	12,092	4,841,799	2,911	4,554,564	25,811	1,259,779
finance & insurance	30,041	6,957,300	5,475	5,156,548	25,554	1,354,715
professional, scientific & technical services	154,235	27,211,001	29,995	23,336,678	195,841	9,952,081
health care & social assistance	123,689	29,929,830	44,890	26,661,428	279,781	10,304,495
services	188,673	11,265,526	30,816	7,185,076	113,216	2,004,081
industries not classified	1,201	207,783	1,201	207,783	1,555	33,713

SOURCE: U.S. Bureau of the Census, 2002 Economic Census Survey of Business Owners: Asian-Owned Firms; SB02-00CS-ASIAN, "(Table 1) Statistics for Asian-Owned Firms by Kind of Business and Detailed Group: 2002", issued May 2006.

NOTES: Data from the 2002 Economic Census. 'Asian' as shown is equivalent to 'Asian Alone'. 'Native Hawaiian and Pacific Islander' is categorized separately.

UNITS: Firms in number of firms; sales and receipts in thousands of dollars; employees in number of employees; annual payroll in thousands of dollars.

Table 10.11 Asian-Owned Firms, by State, 2002

	all firms		firms with paid employees			
	firms	sales & receipts	firms	sales & receipts	employees	annual payroll
United States	1,104,189	$326,352,983	319,295	$290,805,663	2,212,813	$55,991,382
Alabama	4,269	1,491,205	1,621	1,351,301	14,527	363,784
Alaska	1,908	421,147	630	362,842	5,222	93,176
Arizona	10,215	2,395,790	3,183	2,084,027	24,405	499,151
Arkansas	2,052	613,396	916	566,899	7,096	109,798
California	371,415	125,606,279	102,517	111,599,113	745,300	19,035,160
Colorado	10,910	2,450,916	3,441	2,156,326	21,343	500,075
Connecticut	7,170	1,862,697	2,444	1,547,446	13,139	361,612
Delaware	1,895	617,928	776	554,474	3,877	110,511
District of Columbia	2,411	1,002,718	1,366	na	na	na
Florida	41,275	11,207,521	13,596	10,070,849	91,306	1,965,003
Georgia	26,916	7,979,379	9,467	7,150,712	54,533	1,216,133
Hawaii	44,969	12,587,869	10,329	11,251,449	92,218	2,417,758
Idaho	1,111	283,886	427	263,278	2,837	42,870
Illinois	44,480	14,556,520	13,281	13,378,486	98,344	2,723,063
Indiana	6,077	2,583,779	2,318	2,425,644	20,422	508,450
Iowa	1,776	452,509	695	406,401	5,479	107,340
Kansas	3,564	897,740	1,407	819,308	8,535	171,536
Kentucky	3,236	1,362,528	1,296	1,291,638	11,966	290,084
Louisiana	8,218	1,793,668	2,405	1,478,888	17,376	282,745
Maine	834	204,733	431	186,293	2,365	35,245
Maryland	26,309	7,052,097	7,736	6,317,502	50,438	1,519,152
Massachusetts	18,063	5,016,309	5,353	4,500,097	37,185	1,206,463
Michigan	15,286	5,110,999	5,195	4,615,260	44,587	1,440,425
Minnesota	7,700	1,775,531	1,828	1,560,982	16,887	402,333
Mississippi	2,914	1,215,166	1,060	1,068,203	9,215	158,073
Missouri	6,380	1,883,012	2,524	1,747,134	15,170	331,427
Montana	512	100,254	256	93,021	1,519	26,166
Nebraska	1,456	685,646	615	655,489	6,191	136,967
Nevada	8,872	1,988,575	2,264	1,646,654	12,713	315,449
New Hampshire	1,528	403,642	659	343,252	4,119	89,811
New Jersey	51,948	18,493,492	16,868	16,932,870	85,125	2,807,554
New Mexico	2,364	631,309	870	576,289	7,508	152,216

continued on the next page

Table 10.11 continued

	all firms		firms with paid employees			
	firms	sales & receipts	firms	sales & receipts	employees	annual payroll
New York	145,519	$30,433,897	34,844	$26,405,412	164,334	$4,426,300
North Carolina	13,694	3,505,565	4,487	3,134,758	32,759	627,395
North Dakota	277	107,622	161	103,432	1,466	17,815
Ohio	13,740	5,106,036	5,452	4,667,865	42,955	1,201,652
Oklahoma	4,587	929,155	1,534	786,565	9,452	174,798
Oregon	9,053	2,181,567	2,850	1,845,829	22,714	405,313
Pennsylvania	22,627	6,537,611	7,186	5,841,219	42,738	1,233,054
Rhode Island	1,544	324,001	434	280,470	2,612	67,937
South Carolina	4,410	2,055,405	1,858	1,922,823	14,968	264,746
South Dakota	300	87,632	93	82,652	582	13,683
Tennessee	7,241	2,182,650	2,753	1,964,852	21,971	375,507
Texas	77,980	20,565,989	21,754	18,072,734	176,407	3,792,990
Utah	2,821	706,979	885	625,371	7,145	140,944
Vermont	433	66,965	185	na	na	na
Virginia	30,462	7,700,234	8,235	6,856,273	70,033	2,048,146
Washington	26,880	7,115,430	8,139	6,341,047	44,828	1,063,635
West Virginia	1,234	435,064	653	411,101	4,329	137,699
Wisconsin	4,956	1,498,511	1,809	1,358,535	11,603	320,574
Wyoming	401	84,433	217	77,999	1,237	18,213

SOURCE: U.S. Bureau of the Census, 2002 Economic Census Survey of Business Owners: Asian-Owned Firms; SB02-00CS-ASIAN, "(Table 2) Statistics for Asian-Owned Firms by State and Kind of Business: 2002", issued May 2006.

NOTES: Data from the 2002 Economic Census. 'Asian' as shown is equivalent to 'Asian Alone'. 'Native Hawaiian and Pacific Islander' is categorized separately.

UNITS: Firms in number of firms; sales and receipts in thousands of dollars; employees in number of employees; annual payroll in thousands of dollars.

Table 10.12 Small Business Administration Loans to Minority Small Businesses, 1990 – 2004

	Asian	Total Minority
1990		
Number of loans	1,075	2,367
Amount ($ mil.)	$317	$576
2000		
Number of loans	5,838	11,999
Amount ($ mil.)	$2,383	$3,634
2002		
Number of loans	7,249	14,305
Amount ($ mil.)	$2,799	$4,228
2003		
Number of loans	9,507	20,182
Amount ($ mil.)	$2,756	$4,215
2004		
Number of loans	12,100	25,406
Amount ($ mil.)	$3,399	$5,143

SOURCE: U.S. Census Bureau, Statistical Abstract of the United States: 2006; p. 517, table 745.

NOTES: 'Asian' refers to 'Asian American.'

UNITS: Amount in millions of dollars.

Table 10.13 Summary of Results of the 2004 Consumer Expenditure Survey

	Asian consumer units	White consumer units	All consumer units
Number of consumer units	3,957	98,552	116,282
income before taxes	$67,705	$56,150	$54,453
age of referenced person	41.7	49.0	48.5
Average number in consumer unit:			
persons	2.8	2.4	2.5
children under 18 years old	0.7	0.6	0.6
persons 65 and over	0.2	0.3	0.3
earners	1.5	1.3	1.3
vehicles	1.7	2.0	1.9
percent homeowner	58%	71%	68%
Average annual expenditures			
Total	$49,459	$44,962	$43,395
food	6,742	5,958	5,781
food at home	3,689	3,418	3,347
- cereals and bakery products	527	469	461
- meats, poultry, fish, and eggs	1,021	872	880
- dairy products	286	391	371
- fruits and vegetables	870	566	561
- other food at home	985	1,121	1,075
food away from home	3,053	2,539	2,434
alcoholic beverages	325	505	459
housing	17,418	14,181	13,918
shelter	11,728	8,071	7,998
- owned dwellings	7,734	5,530	5,324
- rented dwellings	3,537	2,022	2,201
- other lodging	458	519	473
utilities, fuels and public services	2,781	2,938	2,927
household operations	885	788	753
housekeeping supplies	472	630	594
household furnishings and equipment	1,552	1,754	1,646
apparel and services	1,885	1,821	1,816

continued on the next page

Table 10.13 continued

	Asian consumer units	White consumer units	All consumer units
transportation	8,556	8,166	7,801
- vehicle purchases	3,676	3,615	3,397
- gasoline and motor oil	1,637	1,647	1,598
- other vehicle expenses	2,330	2,460	2,365
- public transportation	913	443	441
health care	2,101	2,762	2,574
entertainment	1,789	2,401	2,218
personal care products and services	506	595	581
reading	112	142	130
education	2,087	904	905
tobacco products and smoking supplies	103	308	288
miscellaneous	569	728	690
cash contributions	1,089	1,501	1,408
personal insurance and pensions	6,176	4,991	4,823
- life and other personal insurance	306	408	390
- pensions and Social Security	5,871	4,584	4,433

SOURCE: U.S. Department of Labor, Bureau of Labor Statistics, Consumer Expenditure Survey, 2004, table 7, issued April 2006.

NOTES: 'All consumer units' includes consumer units of Total.

UNITS: Number of consumer units in thousands; average numbers as shown; average annual expenditures by category, averages in current dollars.

Glossary

ACUTE CONDITION see **CONDITION (HEALTH).**

AGE ADJUSTMENT

Age adjustment, using the direct method, is the application of the age specific rates in a population of interest to a standardized age distribution in order to eliminate the differences in observed rates that result from age differences in population composition. This adjustment is usually done when comparing two or more populations at one point in time, or one population at two or more points in time.

AGGRAVATED ASSAULT see **CRIME**.

ARSON see **CRIME**.

AVERAGE see **MEAN; MEDIAN**.

BED (HOSPITAL; NURSING HOME)

Any bed that is staffed for use by inpatients is counted as a bed in a facility.

BED-DISABILITY DAY see **DISABILITY DAY**.

BIRTH see **LIVE BIRTH**.

BURGLARY see **CRIME**.

CAUSE OF DEATH

For the purpose of national mortality statistics, every death is attributed to one underlying condition, based on information reported on the death certificate and utilizing the international rules (International Classifications of Disease) for selecting the underlying cause of death from reported conditions. Selected causes of death are shown on tables.

CHRONIC CONDITION see **CONDITION (HEALTH)**.

CIVILIAN LABOR FORCE

All persons (excluding members of the Armed Forces) who are either employed or unemployed. (The experienced civilian labor force is a subgroup of the civilian labor force, composed of all persons, employed and unemployed, that have worked before.)

Employed persons are those persons 16 years old and over who were either a) "at work"- those who did any work at all as paid employees, or in their own business or profession, or on their own farm, or worked 15 or more hours as unpaid workers on a family farm or in a family business; or b) "with a job but not at work"- those who did not work during the reference period but had jobs or businesses from which they were temporarily absent due to illness, bad weather, industrial dispute, vacation, or other personal reasons. Excluded from the employed are persons whose only activity consisted of work around the house or volunteer work for religious, charitable, and similar organizations.

Employed persons are classified as either **full-time workers**, those who worked 35 hours or more per week; or **part-time workers**, those who worked less than 35 hours per week.

Unemployed persons are those who were neither "at work" nor "with a job, but not at work" and who were a) looking for work, and b) available to accept a job. Also included as unemployed are persons who are waiting to be called back to a job from which they have been laid off. The unemployed are divided into four groups according to reason for unemployment:

--**job losers** (including those who have been laid off)
--**job leavers** who have left their job voluntarily
--**reentrants**, persons who have worked before and are reentering the labor force
--**new entrants** to the labor force looking for work

CIVILIAN NONINSTITUTIONAL POPULATION see **POPULATION**.

CIVILIAN POPULATION see **POPULATION**.

COLLEGE

A postsecondary school which offers a general or liberal arts education, usually leading to an associate, bachelor's, master's, doctor's, or first professional degree. Junior colleges and community colleges are included. See also **Institution of Higher Education; University.**

COMMUNITY HOSPITAL

All non-federal short term hospitals, excluding hospital units of institutions, whose services are available to the public. **Short term hospitals** are those where the average length of stay is less than 30 days.

CONDITION (HEALTH)

A health condition is a departure from a state of physical or mental well-being. Based on duration, there are two categories of conditions: acute and chronic.

An **acute condition** is one that has lasted less than three months, and has involved either a physician visit (medical attention) or restricted activity.

A **chronic condition** is any condition lasting three months or more, or is one classified as chronic regardless of the time of onset. See also **Health Limitation of Activity.**

CONSUMER EXPENDITURE SURVEY

A survey of current consumer expenditures reflecting the buying habits of American consumers. Begun in 1979 and conducted jointly by the U.S. Bureau of Labor Statistics and the U.S. Bureau of the Census, the survey consists of two parts: an interview panel survey in which the expenditures of consumer units are obtained in five interviews conducted every three months, and a diary or record keeping survey completed by the participating households for two consecutive one-week periods. See also **Consumer Unit.**

The Consumer Expenditure Survey, which collects data on expenditures, should not be confused with the Consumer Price Index, which measures the average change in prices of consumer goods and services.

CONSUMER UNIT

An entity used as the basis of the Consumer Expenditure Survey. A consumer unit comprises either

--all the members of a particular household who are related by blood, marriage, adoption, or other legal arrangements; or

--a person living alone or sharing a household with others, or living as a roomer in a private home or lodging house or in a permanent living quarters in a hotel or motel, but who is financially independent; or

--two or more persons living together who pool their income to make joint expenditure decisions.

A consumer unit may or may not be a household.

CRIME

A crime is an action which is prohibited by law. Their are two major statistical programs which measure crime in the United States. The first is the Uniform Crime Reporting (UCR) program, administered by the FBI. The Bureau receives monthly and annual reports from most police agencies around the country (covering more than 93% of the population). These reports contain information on eight major types of crime (called collectively, serious crime), which are known to police. Serious crime consists of four violent crimes (murder and non-negligent manslaughter, which includes willful felonious homicides and is based on police investigations rather than determinations of a medical examiner; forcible rape, which includes attempted rape; robbery, which includes stealing or taking anything of value by force or violence, or by threat of force or violence, and includes attempted robbery; and aggravated assault which includes intent to kill), and four property crimes (burglary, which includes any unlawful entry to commit a felony or theft and includes attempted burglary and burglary followed by larceny; larceny, which includes theft of property or articles of value without use of force, violence, or fraud, and excludes embezzlement, con games, forgery, etc.; motor vehicle theft, which includes all cases where vehicles are driven away and abandoned, but excludes vehicles taken for temporary use and returned by the taker; and arson, which includes any willful or malicious burning or attempt to burn, with or without the intent to defraud, of a dwelling house, public building, motor vehicle, aircraft, or personal property of another.)

The second approach to the measurement of crime is through the National Crime Survey (NCS) administered by the Bureau of Justice Statistics. The survey is based on a representative sample of approximately 49,000 households, inhabited by about 102,000 persons age 12 and over. Although the categories of crime are similar to those used by the FBI in the UCR, the NCS is based on reports of victimization directly by victims, as opposed to crimes reported to police as in the UCR. As might be imagined, not all crimes are reported or known to police, therefore NCS estimates of crime tend to be significantly higher than UCR figures. The NCS also differs from the UCR in that only crimes whose victims can be interviewed are included (hence there are no homicide statistics), and only victims who are 12 years old or older are counted. The two central concepts in the NCS are victimization, which is the specific criminal act as it affects a single victim, and a criminal incident, which is a specific criminal act involving one or more victims. Thus in regard to personal crime, there are more victimizations than incidents.

DEATH see **CAUSE OF DEATH; INFANT MORTALITY**.

DISABILITY

The presence of a physical, mental, or other health condition which has lasted six or more months and which limits or prevents a particular type of activity. See also **Work Disability.**

DISABILITY DAY

A day on which a person's usual activity is reduced because of illness or injury. There are four types of disability days (which are not mutually exclusive). They are

--a **restricted-activity day**, a day on which a person cuts down on his or her usual activities because of illness or an injury.

--a **bed-disability day,** a day on which a person stays in bed more than half of the daylight hours (or normal waking hours) because of a specific illness or injury. All hospital days are bed-disability days. Bed disability days may also be work-loss days or school loss days.

--a **work-loss day**, a day on which a person did not work at his or her job or business for at least half of his or her normal workday because of a specific illness or injury. Work loss days are determined only for employed persons.

--a **school-loss day**, a day on which a child did not attend school for at least half of his or her normal schoolday because of a specific illness or injury. School-loss days are determined only for children 6 to 16 years of age.

DISPOSABLE INCOME see **INCOME.**

EMPLOYED PERSONS see **CIVILIAN LABOR FORCE**.

EMPLOYMENT STATUS see **LABOR FORCE STATUS**.

ENROLLMENT

The total number of students registered in a given school unit at a given time, generally in the fall of the year. See also **Full-Time Enrollment; Part-Time Enrollment.**

EVER MARRIED PERSONS see **MARITAL STATUS**.

EXPERIENCED CIVILIAN LABOR FORCE

That portion of the Civilian Labor Force, both employed and unemployed, that have worked before. Excludes new entrants to the Civilian Labor Force. See also **Civilian Labor Force.**

EXPERIENCED WORKER see **EXPERIENCED CIVILIAN LABOR FORCE**.

FAMILY

A type (subgroup) of household in which there are two or more persons living together (including the householder) who are related by birth, marriage, or adoption. All such related persons in one housing unit are considered as members of one family. (For example, if the son or daughter of the family householder and that son's or daughter's spouse and/or children are members of the household, they are all counted as part of the householder's family.) However, non-family members who are not related to the householder (such as a roomer or boarder and his or her spouse, or a resident employee and his or her spouse who are living in), are not counted as family members but as unrelated individuals living in a family household. Thus for Census purposes, a housing unit can contain only one household, and a household can contain only one family. See also **Family Type; Household; Householder; Unrelated Individual.**

FAMILY INCOME see **INCOME**.

FAMILY TYPE

Families are classified by type according to the sex of the householder and the presence of a spouse and children. The three main types of households are: **Married Couples,** in which a husband and wife live together (with or without other persons in the household); **Male Householder, No Wife Present,** in which a male householder lives together with other members of his family but without a wife; and **Female Householder, No Husband Present,** in which a female householder lives together with other members of her family but without a husband. See also **Family; Household.**

FARM

As defined by the Bureau of the Census (and adopted by the Department of Agriculture), a farm is any place from which $1,000 or more of agricultural products were sold, or would have been sold during a given year. Control of the farm may be exercised through ownership or management, or through a lease, rental or cropping arrangement. In the case of landowners who have one or more tenants or renters, the land operated by each is counted as a separate farm. This definition has been in effect since 1974.

FARMLAND

All land under the control of a farm operator, including land not actually under cultivation or not used for pasture or grazing. Rent free land is included as part of a farm only if the operator has sole use of it. Land used for pasture or grazing on a per head basis that is neither owned nor leased by the farm operator is not included except for grazing lands controlled by grazing associations leased on a per acre basis.

FARM INCOME

Gross farm income comprises cash receipts from farm marketings of crops and livestock, federal government payments made directly to farmers for farm-related activities, rental value of farm homes, value of farm products consumed in farm homes, and other farm-related income such as machine hire and custom work.

FULL-TIME ENROLLMENT (HIGHER EDUCATION)

The number of students enrolled in higher education courses with a total credit load equal to at least 75% of the normal full-time course load.

FULL-TIME WORKERS see **CIVILIAN LABOR FORCE**.

HATE CRIME

A hate crime, also known as a bias crime, is a criminal offense committed against a person, property, or society that is motivated, in whole or in part, by the offender's bias against a race, religion, disability, sexual orientation, or ethnicity/national origin.

HEALTH LIMITATION OF ACTIVITY

A characteristic of persons with chronic conditions. Each person identified as having a chronic condition is classified as to the extent to which his or her activities are limited by the condition as follows:

--persons unable to carry on a major activity (that is the principal activity of a person of his or her age-sex group: for persons 1-5 years of age, it refers to ordinary play with other children; for persons 6-16 years of age, it refers to school attendance; for persons 17 years of age and over, it usually refers to a job, housework, or school attendance.)

--persons limited in the amount or kind of major activity performed.

--persons not limited in major activity, but otherwise limited.

--persons not limited in activity.

See also **Condition (Health).**

HEALTH MAINTENANCE ORGANIZATION (HMO)

A prepaid health plan delivering comprehensive care to members through designated providers, having a fixed monthly payment for health care services, and requiring members to be in the plan for a specified period of time (usually one year). HMOs are distinguished by the relationship of the providers to the plan. HMO model types are: **Group** -- an HMO that delivers health services through a physician group controlled by the HMO, or an HMO that contracts with one or more independent group practices to provide health services; **Individual Practice Association (IPA)** -- an HMO that contracts directly with physicians in independent practice, and/or contracts with one or more associations of physicians in independent practice, and/or contracts with one or more multi-specialty group practices (but the plan is predominantly organized around solo-single specialty practices).

HIGHER EDUCATION see **INSTITUTION OF HIGHER EDUCATION**.

HISPANIC ORIGIN

An aspect of a person's ancestry. The Bureau of the Census in many of its survey asks persons if they are of Hispanic origin. There are four main subcategories of Hispanic origin: Mexican, Puerto Rican, Cuban, and other Hispanic. Hispanic origin is not a racial classification. Persons may be of any race and of Hispanic origin. Hispanic origin is used interchangeably with Spanish and Spanish origin.

HOSPITAL see **COMMUNITY HOSPITAL**.

HOSPITAL DAY

A hospital day is a night spent in a hospital by a person admitted as an inpatient.

HOUSEHOLD

The person or persons occupying a housing unit. There are two main types of households: family households, which consist of two or more persons related by birth, marriage, or adoption living together (see also **Family; Family Type**); and non-family households, which consist of a person living alone, or together with unrelated individuals (see Unrelated Individuals). See also **Householder.**

HOUSEHOLD INCOME see **INCOME**.

HOUSEHOLD TYPE see **HOUSEHOLD**.

HOUSEHOLDER

The person in whose name a housing unit is rented or owned.

INCIDENT see **CRIME**.

INCOME

The term income has different definitions depending on how it is modified and in what situation it is used. Like many government statistical terms, income can be viewed hierarchically.

Personal income is the current income received by persons from all sources, minus their personal contributions for social insurance. Persons include individuals (including owners of unincorporated firms), non-profit institutions serving individuals, private trust funds, and private non-insured welfare funds. Personal income includes transfers (payments not resulting from current production) from government and business such as Social Security benefits, public assistance, etc., but excludes transfers among persons. Also included are certain non-monetary types of income, chiefly estimated net rental value to owner-occupants of their homes, the value of services furnished without payment by financial intermediaries, and food and fuel produced and consumed on farms.

Disposable personal income is personal income less personal tax and non-tax payments. It is income available to persons for spending and saving. Personal tax and non-tax payments are tax payments (net of refunds) by persons (excluding contributions for social insurance) that are not chargeable to business expenses, and certain personal payments to general government that are treated like taxes. Personal taxes include income, estate and gift, personal property, and motor vehicle licenses. Non-tax payments include passport fees, fines and penalties, donations, tuition and fees paid to schools and hospitals mainly operated by the government.

Money income is a smaller, less inclusive category than personal income. Money income is the sum of the amounts received from wages and salaries, self-employment income (including losses), Social Security, Supplemental Security Income, public assistance, interest, dividends, rents, royalties, estate or trust income, veterans payments, unemployment and workers' compensation payments, private and government retirement and disability pensions, alimony, child support, and any other source of money income which was regularly received. Capital gains or losses and lump-sum or one-time payments, such as life insurance settlements, are excluded. Also excluded are non-cash benefits such as food stamps, health benefits, housing subsidies, rent-free housing, and the goods produced and consumed on farms. Money income is reported for households and various household types as well as for unrelated individuals. (In regard to family money income it should be noted that only the amount received by all family members 15 years old and over is counted, and excludes income received by household members not related to the householder.) It is reported in aggregate, median, mean, and per capita amounts. Money income is also used for determining the poverty status of families and unrelated individuals.

INFANT MORTALITY

The deaths of live-born children who do not reach their first birthday. Infant mortality is usually expressed as a rate per 1,000 live births.

INSTITUTION OF HIGHER EDUCATION

An institution which offers programs of study beyond the secondary school level terminating in an associate, baccalaureate, or higher degree. See also **College; University.**

JAIL

A facility, usually operated by a local law enforcement agency, holding persons detained pending adjudication and/or persons committed after adjudication to a sentence of one year or less.

LABOR FORCE STATUS

A term which refers to whether or not a person is in the labor force, and, if in the labor force, whether he or she is employed or unemployed, a full-time worker or a part-time worker, etc. Persons are in the labor force if they are in the civilian labor force or in the Armed Forces.

The civilian labor force consists of both employed and unemployed persons, full-time and part-time workers. Generally, persons outside the labor force consist of full-time homemakers, students who do not work, retired persons, and inmates of institutions. "Discouraged workers," those who do not have a job and have not been seeking one, are also considered to be not in the labor force. See also **Civilian Labor Force.**

LARCENY see **CRIME**.

LIMITATION OF ACTIVITY see **HEALTH LIMITATION OF ACTIVITY**.

LIVE BIRTH

The live birth of an infant, defined as the complete expulsion or extraction from its mother of a product of conception, irrespective of the duration of the pregnancy, which, after such separation, breathes or shows any evidence of life such as heartbeat, umbilical cord pulsation, or definite movement of voluntary muscles, whether or not the umbilical cord has been cut or the placenta is attached. Each such birth is considered live born.

MARITAL STATUS

All persons 15 years of age and older are classified by the Bureau of the Census according to marital status. The Bureau defines two broad categories of marital status: **Single** - all those persons who have never been married (including persons whose marriage has been annulled), and **Ever married** - which is composed of the now married, the widowed, and the divorced. **Now married** persons are those who are legally married (as well as some persons who have common law marriages, along with some unmarried couples who live together and report their marital status as married), and whose marriage has not ended by widowhood or divorce. The now married are sometimes further subdivided: married, spouse present; separated; married, spouse absent; married, spouse absent, other. **Married, spouse present** covers married couples living together. **Separated** includes those persons legally separated or otherwise absent from their spouse because of marital discord (such as persons who have been deserted or who have parted because they no longer want to live together but who have not obtained a divorce). Separated includes persons with a limited divorce. **Married, spouse absent** covers those households where the both the husband and the wife were not counted as members of the same household, (or where both husband and wife lived together in group quarters). **Married, spouse absent, other**, includes those married persons whose spouse was not counted as a member of the same household, besides those who are separated. Included are persons whose spouse was employed and living away from home, absent in the armed forces, or was an inmate of an institution. **Widowed** includes widows and widowers who have not remarried. **Divorced** includes persons who are legally divorced and have not remarried.

MARRIED COUPLES see **FAMILY TYPE**.

MARRIED PERSONS see **MARITAL STATUS**.

MEAN

The arithmetic average of a set of values. It is derived by dividing the sum of a group of numerical items by the total number of items. Mean income (of a population), for example, is defined as the value obtained by dividing the total or aggregate income by the population. Thus, the mean income for families is obtained by dividing the aggregate of all income reported by persons in families by the total number of families. See also **Median.**

MEDIAN

In general, a value that divides the total range of values into two equal parts. For example, to say that the median money income of families in the United States in 1985 was $27,735 indicates that half of all families had incomes larger than that value, and half had less. See also **Mean.**

MEDICAID

A federally funded but state administered and operated program which provides medical benefits to certain low income persons in need of medical care. The program, authorized in 1965 by Title XIX of the Social Security Act, categorically covers participants in the Aid to Families with Dependent Children (AFDC) program, as well as some participants in the Supplemental Security Income (SSI) program, along with those other people deemed medically needy in each participating state. Each state determines the benefits covered, rates of payment to providers, and methods of administering the program.

MEDICARE

A federally funded nationwide health insurance program providing health insurance protection to people 65 years of age and over, people eligible for social security disability payments for more than two years, and people with end-state renal disease, regardless of income. The program was enacted July 30, 1965, as title XVIII, Health Insurance for the Aged, of the Social Security Act, and became effective on July 1, 1966. It consists of two separate but coordinated programs: hospital insurance (Part A), and supplementary medical insurance (Part B).

MONEY INCOME see **INCOME**.

MURDER see **CRIME.**

NATIONAL CRIME SURVEY

A twice yearly survey of 49,000 households comprising over 102,000 inhabitants 12 years of age and older. Administered by the Bureau of Justice Statistics, the survey measures criminal victimization by surveying victims directly. It differs from the FBI Uniform Crime Report (UCR) which is based on crimes reported to police. See also **Crime.**

OCCUPATION

The kind of work a person does at a job or business. Occupation is reported for a given survey period, (most frequently the period covered by the survey, the reference period, is the week including March 12). If the person was not at work during the reference period, occupation usually refers to the person's most recent job or business. Persons working at more than one job are asked to identify the job at which he or she works the most hours, which is then counted as his or her occupation.

Occupations are classified according to the Standard Occupational Classification system (SOC), a system promulgated by the federal Office of Management and Budget.

PART-TIME ENROLLMENT (HIGHER EDUCATION)

The number of students enrolled in higher education courses with a total credit load of less than 75% of the normal full-time credit load.

PART-TIME WORKERS see **CIVILIAN LABOR FORCE**.

PERSONAL INCOME see **INCOME**.

POPULATION

The number of inhabitants of an area. The total population of the United States is the sum of all persons living within the United States, plus all members of the Armed Forces living in foreign countries, Puerto Rico, Guam, and the U.S. Virgin Islands. Other Americans living abroad (e.g., civilian federal employees and dependents of members of the Armed Forces or other federal employees) are not included.

The **resident population of the United States** is the population living within the geographic United States. This includes members of the Armed Forces stationed in the United States and their families, as well as foreigners working or studying here. It excludes foreign military, naval, and diplomatic personnel and their families located here and residing in embassies or similar quarters, as well as Americans living abroad. Resident population is often the denominator when calculating birth and death rates, incidence of disease, and other rates.

The **civilian population** is the resident population excluding members of the Armed Forces. However, families of members of the Armed Forces are included.

The **civilian non-institutional population** is the civilian population not residing in institutions. Institutions include correctional institutions; detention homes and training schools for juvenile delinquents; homes for the aged and dependent (e.g., nursing homes and convalescent homes); homes for dependent and neglected children; homes and schools for the mentally and physically handicapped; homes for unwed mothers; psychiatric, tuberculosis, and chronic disease hospitals; and residential treatment centers.

POVERTY STATUS

Although the term poverty connotes a complex set of economic, social, and psychological conditions, the standard statistical definition provides for only estimates of economic poverty. These are based on the receipt of money income before taxes and exclude the value of government payments and transfers such as food stamps or Medicare; private transfers, such as health insurance premiums paid by employers; gifts; the depletion of assets; and borrowed money. Thus the term poverty as used by government agencies, classifies persons and families in relation to being above or below a specified income level, or poverty threshold. Those below this threshold are said to be in poverty, or more accurately, as below the poverty level. Poverty thresholds vary by size of family, number of children, and age of householder and are updated annually. Poverty status is also determined for unrelated individuals living in households, but not for those living in group quarters nor for persons in the Armed Forces. The poverty threshold is revised each year according to formula based on the Consumer Price Index.

PRISON

A confinement facility having custodial authority over adults sentenced to confinement for a period of more than one year. Prisons are usually run by state or federal authorities.

PRIVATE SCHOOL see **SCHOOL**.

PROPERTY CRIME see **CRIME**.

PUBLIC SCHOOL see **SCHOOL**.

RACE

The Bureau of the Census in many of its surveys (most notably in the decennial censuses of population) asks all persons to identify themselves according to race. The concept of race as used by the Bureau reflects the self-identification of the respondents. It is not meant to denote any clear cut scientific or biological definition.

Although it is often reported with racial categories, **Hispanic origin**, or Spanish origin, is not a racial category. Persons may be of any race and of Hispanic origin. Those who describe themselves as Hispanic (or Mexican, Cuban, Chicano, etc.) in response to a question about race, are included by the Bureau in the racial classification, "other." See also **Hispanic Origin.**

RAPE see **CRIME**.

REFERENCE PERSON

Most frequently, the person who responds to a government survey. Most surveys done by the federal government are based on households and begin by asking the initial respondent the name of the person in whose name the housing unit is owned or rented (this person is designated as the householder). Usually the householder is the reference person. Other household members are defined in relation to the householder.

REGION

The Bureau of the Census has divided the United States into four regions. This division is the primary geographic subdivision of the nation for statistical reporting purposes. As a result, almost all federal agencies, along with many private data collectors, have adopted the regional subdivision and use it for presenting statistical data. The four regions are the **Northeast** (Maine, New Hampshire, Vermont, Massachusetts, Rhode Island, Connecticut, New York, New Jersey, Pennsylvania); the **Midwest** (Ohio, Indiana, Illinois, Michigan, Wisconsin, Minnesota, Iowa, Missouri, North Dakota, South Dakota, Kansas, Nebraska); the **South** (Delaware, Maryland, District of Columbia, Virginia, West Virginia, North Carolina, South Carolina, Georgia, Florida, Kentucky, Tennessee, Alabama, Mississippi, Arkansas, Louisiana, Oklahoma, Texas); and the **West** (Montana, Idaho, Colorado, Wyoming, New Mexico, Arizona, Utah, Nevada, Washington, Oregon, California, Alaska, Hawaii). In this book, all regional data conform to this definition.

REGULAR SCHOOL see **SCHOOL**.

RESIDENT POPULATION see **POPULATION**.

RESTRICTED-ACTIVITY DAY see **DISABILITY DAY**.

ROBBERY see **CRIME**.

SCHOOL

Elementary and secondary schools are divisions of the school system consisting of students in one or more grade groups or other identifiable groups, organized as one unit with one or more teachers giving instruction of a defined type, and housed in a school plant of one or more buildings. More than one school may be housed in one school plant as is the case where elementary and secondary programs are housed in the same building.

Regular schools generally are those which advance a person toward a diploma or degree. They include public and private nursery schools, kindergartens, graded schools, colleges, universities, and professional schools.

Public schools are controlled and supported by local, state, or federal government agencies.

Private schools are controlled and supported mainly by religious organizations, private persons, or private organizations.

SCHOOL ENROLLMENT see **ENROLLMENT**.

SCHOOL-LOSS DAY see **DISABILITY DAY**.

SELF-EMPLOYMENT INCOME

A type of money income which comprises net income (gross receipts minus operating expenses) received by persons from an unincorporated business, profession, and/or from the operation of a farm as a farm owner, tenant, or sharecropper. See also **Money Income.**

SEPARATED PERSONS see **MARITAL STATUS**.

SERIOUS CRIME see **CRIME**.

SINGLE PERSON HOUSEHOLDS see **HOUSEHOLD**.

SINGLE PERSONS see **MARITAL STATUS**.

UNEMPLOYED PERSONS see **CIVILIAN LABOR FORCE**.

UNEMPLOYMENT see **CIVILIAN LABOR FORCE**.

UNIFORM CRIME REPORTING (UCR) PROGRAM

A program administered by the FBI which collects reports from most police agencies in the nation (covering more than 93% of the population) on serious crimes known to police (violent crime and property crime), arrests, police officers and related items. The Bureau issues monthly and annual summary reports based on the program. See also **Crime.**

UNIVERSITY

An institution of higher education consisting of a liberal arts college, a diverse graduate program, and usually two or more professional schools or faculties and empowered to confer degrees in various fields of study. See also **Higher Education.**

UNRELATED INDIVIDUAL

An unrelated individual is generally a person living in a household, and is either: 1) a householder living alone or only with persons who are not related to him or her by blood, marriage, or adoption, or; 2) a roomer, boarder, partner, roommate, or resident employee unrelated to the householder. Certain persons living in group quarters (who are not inmates of institutions) are also counted as unrelated individuals.

VICTIMIZATION see **CRIME**.

VIOLENT CRIME see **CRIME**.

VOTING AGE POPULATION

All persons over the age of 18 (the voting age for federal elections) in a given geographic area comprise the voting age population. The voting age population does include a small number of persons who, although of voting age, are not eligible to vote (e.g. resident aliens, inmates of institutions, etc.). The voting age population is estimated in even numbered years by the Bureau of the Census.

WAGES AND SALARIES

Wages and salaries are a type (subgroup) of money income and include civilian wages and salaries, Armed Forces pay and allowances, piece-rate payments, commissions, tips, National Guard or Reserve pay (received for training periods), and cash bonuses before deductions for taxes, pensions, union dues, etc. See also **Money Income.**

WIDOWED PERSONS see **MARITAL STATUS**.

WORK DISABILITY

A health condition which limits the kind or amount of work a person can do, or prevents working at a job. A person is limited in the kind of work he or she can do if the person has a health condition which restricts his or her choice of jobs. A person is limited in amount of work if he or she is not able to work at a full-time (35 hours or more per week) job or business. See also **Condition (Health).**

WORK-LOSS DAY see **DISABILITY DAY**.

Index